A Devil's Dictionary
of Business Jargon

A Devil's Dictionary of BUSINESS JARGON

David Olive

KEY PORTER BOOKS

Copyright © 2001 by David Olive

All rights reserved. No part of this work covered by the copyrights hereon may be reproduced or used in any form or by any means—graphic, electronic or mechanical, including photocopying, recording, taping or information storage and retrieval systems—without the prior written permission of the publisher, or in the case of photocopying or other reprographic copying, a license from the Canadian Copyright Licensing Agency.

National Library of Canada Cataloguing in Publication Data

Olive, David, 1957–
  A devil's dictionary of business jargon

ISBN 1-55263-367-5

1. Business—Dictionaries. 2. Business—Humor. 3. English language—Jargon Dictionaries.
4. English language—Euphemism—Dictionaries. 5. Business—Quotations, maxims, etc.

I. Title.

HF1001.O56 2001   650'.03   C2001-901681-6

The Canada Council | Le Conseil des Arts
FOR THE ARTS | DU CANADA
SINCE 1957 | DEPUIS 1957

ONTARIO ARTS COUNCIL
CONSEIL DES ARTS DE L'ONTARIO

The publisher gratefully acknowledges the support of the Canada Council for the Arts and the Ontario Arts Council for its publishing program.

We acknowledge the financial support of the Government of Canada through the Book Publishing Industry Development Program (BPIDP) for our publishing activities.

Key Porter Books Limited
70 The Esplanade
Toronto, Ontario
Canada M5E 1R2
www.keyporter.com

Design: Peter Maher
Electronic formatting: Heidy Lawrance Associates

Printed and bound in Canada

01 02 03 04 05 06 6 5 4 3 2 1

The illustrations on pages 6 and 191 are by Barry Blitt.

For Lynda Sue Bronsten

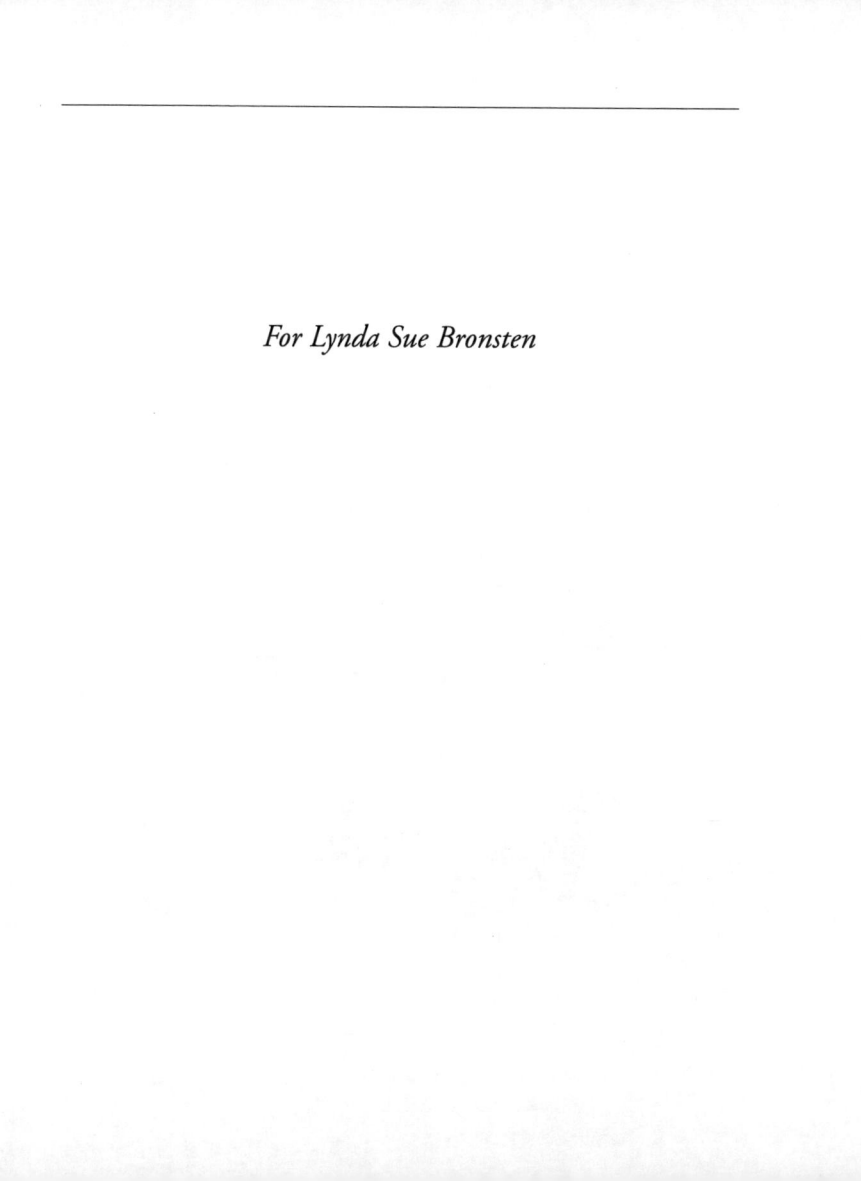

balloon juice
idea hamster
paradigm
buy-in
stress puppy
geek chorus
dead money
blamestorming
face time
vaporware
gadget trance
negative growth
zombie
cyberpseud
puked out
doom loop
trust slug

Contents

Preface *9*

Acknowledgments *15*

A to Z *17*

Index to Quoted Subjects *193*

Preface

With words we govern.
  – Benjamin Disraeli

SELDOM IS CLARITY MORE CALLED FOR THAN IN business, where success depends on summoning the resolve and resources to achieve impossible goals. In the age of horse and carriage, Henry Ford was blessedly direct about his aims: "I will build a motor car for the great multitude, constructed of the best materials, by the best men to be hired, after the simplest designs that modern engineering can devise." So was Bill Gates, some 80 years later, in explaining the mission of a young company then known as Micro-Soft: "A computer on every desk and in every home – and Micro-Soft in every computer."

Such clarity typifies the small start-up operation. Alas, with success comes sprawl — and word gamesmanship. As the worker population of an enterprise grows, employees spend more time managing each other than the business. Managers seem to feel that the people who live in these organizations, which claim the better part of their waking hours, need to be prodded with platitudes, coerced with trite exhortations and jollied along with euphemisms. Direct speech is anathema to leaders with a hidden agenda, and for those with an uncertain grasp of their aims or authority. The modern manager seems to be guided by an aphorism of Charles-Maurice de Talleyrand, the nineteenth-century diplomat, who said that "Speech is a faculty given to man to conceal his thoughts."

When hard times come, managers imagine they can cloak dire threats to the enterprise by speaking of "material adverse conditions." Rather than risk a drop in productivity brought on by layoff-induced anxiety in the ranks, they merely hint at the need for a "census reduction" or an exercise in "head-count realignment."

Shareholders, meanwhile, need to be comforted that management is up to the task of coping with a "challenging economic environment," lest they get the impression they are holding a "roach motel stock" — one that entices investors in good times, and from which they cannot escape when ill fortune strikes.

In good times and bad, people who toil in corporate bureaucracies must deal with the bean-counting "squint," who stifles initiative by withholding budget approval; the "chief table pounder," who spouts "balloon juice" in promoting a pet project that will seal her promotion; and the "seagull manager" who wreaks havoc during a brief stint in a previously untroubled province of the company and then flies away, leaving others to clean up the mess.

The increasingly hectic pace of corporate life gives rise to new species of corporate animals. The "idea hamster" is irrepressible in spinning out impractical concepts, which will be warmly embraced or passionately rejected by the "profundicator," who puts on a show of florid sagacity in pronouncing on subjects both cosmic and trivial. Overworked "cubicle people" racing to meeting unrealistic "drop-dead deadlines" are fated to become either "stress puppies," who embrace the task with overzealous enthusiasm, or "flight risks," who simply mark time as they await an opportunity to defect.

Confusion in the ranks can be traced to the top, where "options junkies" in the executive suite imagine they have empowered front-line employees by increasing their responsibilities but without an accompanying measure of authority or adequate "incentivization." Employees are told to "think outside the box" – a cynical invitation to help the enterprise meet debilitating "stretch goals" by breaking only those rules that don't upset the status quo for their higher-echelon overseers.

The Internet age has given linguistic sorcerers new tools for inflating the importance of prosaic activities. A top U.S.

consulting firm makes a case for the semi-magical nature of its work in motivating mid-level managers by pledging itself to "developing a highly charged yet fluid and networked organization – harnessing, driving, and nurturing the inherent ambiguity and complexity of innovation." The CEO intent on exhibiting his grasp of the new "digibabble," if only for the sake of raising money from venture capital "incubators" of New Economy companies, hypes his "value proposition," his plans for "monetizing" his "aggregated eyeballs" and his innovative "business model" for reaping e-commerce riches with a scheme that is "extensible" and "scalable." His goal is to plant a large "footprint" in a rapidly emerging "space."

"The world is governed more by appearances than by realities," said American statesman and orator Daniel Webster, "so that it is fully necessary to seem to know something as to know it." In the aftermath of the writedown, the sudden stock plunge, the bankruptcy filing or the grisly encounter with regulators and class-action litigants, the patter of too many CEOs and their lieutenants is revealed as a protective covering for an inexpert grasp of the difficulties he or she confronts, or a determined effort to glide through an awkward situation with a glib expression.

Observing the piratic machinations of robber barons and the politicians on their payrolls at the dawn of the twentieth century, journalist and novelist Ambrose Bierce warned readers of his column in *Wasp* magazine about the linguistic treachery of titans in the new industrial age. At age 71, not long after the

1911 appearance of an anthology of those observations in his *Devil's Dictionary*, Bierce departed for Mexico, probably to witness the Pancho Villa revolution, and was not heard from again.

His legacy endures in the *Dictionary*, addressed to those "enlightened souls who prefer dry wines to sweet, sense to sentiment, wit to humor and clean English to slang."

In business, slang has long since given way to more irksome abuses – the hollow rhetoric, polished deceptions and linguistic frauds that collectively fall under the rubric of corpspeak.

This volume is intended as an antidote to the gibberish that passes for current corporate coin, and a handbook for those who seek to assert their own mastery over those who would govern our business enterprises with duplicitous words.

Acknowledgments

I WISH TO THANK THE STAFF OF KEY PORTER BOOKS for their assistance with this book and its predecessor, *White Knights and Poison Pills: A Cynic's Dictionary of Business Jargon*, an earlier volley in the campaign for clarity in business communication. I wish also to acknowledge the inspiring counsel of editors Susan Folkins and Charles Macli, and the generosity of the *National Post* for its support during the completion of the work.

Occasionally, words must serve to veil the facts. But this must happen in such a way that no one becomes aware of it; or, if it should be noticed, excuses must be at hand to be produced immediately.

— NICCOLO MACHIAVELLI,
THE PRINCE

abandonware, *n.* Computer games, applications and operating systems no longer made by their original manufacturers, now floating around the Internet, presumably free of copyright.

academy, company, *n.* A big, old company with a reputation as a "graduate nursery" that trains generalist managers who migrate to top posts at other firms and in the public sector. Alumni, in the case of refugees from General Electric, BP, Procter & Gamble and Unilever, have more clout in corporate and government circles than the output of Oxbridge or Harvard.

accounting, aggressive, *n.* Selective judgment about what to include and leave out of the financial statements. For instance, maybe we can put off until next year any reference to the fire at the uninsured warehouse. And maybe we can include in this year's revenues that big order we're hoping to get in January from whatshisname, the Russian agriculture secretary.

accounts retrievable, *n.* Invoices that bear fruit without the aid of a skip-tracer or small-claims-court action.

acquisition, *n.* Someone else's troubles, cleverly disguised as a remedy for what ails the acquirer. While it's true that most takeovers fail, they at least force management to stop neglecting the original business once the acquisition has soured.

action item, *n.* An issue on which all are agreed that action must be taken. Exactly who is to take the action can be left for a subsequent meeting to determine, by which time the problem ideally will have gone away.

action training, *n.* Training in the field rather than the classroom, on real projects rather than simulations. There comes a point when Deere & Co. grows impatient with MBA graduates who have learned how to sell tractors to fellow classmates, and wonders if they can close a deal with a farmer.

Classroom training is inefficient. Half the people in the room are secretly working on their "real" jobs; half are so relieved not to be doing their real jobs, they've turned their minds off entirely.
 – Management consultant Thomas A. Stewart, in *Fortune* in 2001

actualize, *v.* Get the ball rolling. Time to see if paying customers react the same way to the business plan as colleagues who slept through the PowerPoint presentation.

adminisphere, *n.* The organizational levels above you, populated entirely by dummies who don't know who you are, don't care what you do and have only scorn for your input.

administrative intensity, *n.* Ratio of managers to galley slaves. A successful firm has a low ratio of administrators to "productive head count."

adventure travel, *n.* A trip to see employees at the newly acquired subsidiary, a colonial outpost where head-office visitors are greeted with the same joviality that marked Commodore Perry's first encounter with the Japanese.

after dinner speech, *n.* The unspeakable pursuant to the inedible. Also known as tuxedo unction.

aggregated eyeballs, *n.* The audience for a website, as measured by the number of hits, or page views, it receives. Viewers linger at "sticky," or compelling, sites. If they can be converted from window-shoppers into buyers, they have been "monetized." A media-convergence conglomerate such as AOL Time Warner seeks to "aggregate" eyeballs of *People* readers, HBO subscribers and Warner Bros. ticket buyers. Thus, e-commerce nirvana is an aggregation of sticky monetized eyeballs.

alliance, *n.* A tie that doesn't bind. A tentative partnership between corporations that offers diplomatic immunity for doubters on either side. When used as a stealth courtship, ease of premarital intimacy will determine the prospects of a full-blown merger.

alpha geek, *n.* First among equals in the tech-support crew, and therefore the least user-friendly member of the information technology (IT) staff.

alpha talent, *n.* A software savant or hardware guru who pioneers genuine breakthroughs in technology, leaving it to a mop-up crew of IT drones to make the untried gear actually function in the workplace.

alpha test, *n.* The first trial run, followed by "beta" testing of an improved model that doesn't make that shrieking sound.

ammo-belted, *adj.* Term for a colleague who is armed for interactivity, his apparel bristling with slings and holsters for all his pagers, cell phones, e-mail transponders and digital organizers. The electronic chattel-horse as a fashion statement for the new millennium.

angel investor, *n.* An opportunistic Gabriel no less profit motivated than the average banker, but more imaginative in seeing the money to be made from an unorthodox idea.

Angels don't write the second check. So you better figure out that the company doesn't need a second check. A lot of us lost a lot of zeros in our wealth last year.
– Angel investor Robert H. Lessin of Wit SoundView Group, a venture capital firm

anger expression, *n.* A controlled, constructive outburst in which you are seen to be brave and noble in sticking up for yourself. Full-throated belligerence, by contrast, which marks you as a casualty of "desk rage."

anthropologist, retail, *n.* Student of shoppers' behavior who counsels against putting junk food on high shelves out of reach of kids or placing hearing-aid batteries on low shelves where the elderly are obliged to stoop for them.

apology bonus, *n.* Go-away money for new hires, often recently recruited college grads, from employers suffering an abrupt reversal of fortune. Also known as "reverse hiring bonus" and "preseverance pay" – the employer's bid to keep from being disinvited from future campus job fairs come the next skills-shortage era.

apology, non-apology, *n.* We are, of course, disappointed that a relatively small number of consumers feel they have had an adverse experience with our product. While we know beyond doubt that it is safe when operated properly, except possibly under the most absurd conditions, we deeply regret the circumstance for those few users affected by the unfortunate incidents, which have no connection with our many other fine products.

architect, *v.* The act of embellishing a business plan or an organization chart with pediments, cornices, fretwork and other baroque touches.

We believe that in the nineties, the low-cost position will not come simply from economics of scale, but rather from deliberately architecting an organization and consciously interfacing supplier, customer and key stakeholder relationships.
– Heather Reisman, president of soft-drink bottler Cott Corp., in 1994

aspirational management, *n.* A system that rewards managers for achieving touchy-feely goals in worker empowerment, consensual decision-making, sensitivity training and other programs for helping employees find meaning in the workplace. The system is based on Dr. Harold Lytton-Puzzlewhut's pioneering work with Dengi shepherds in the East Solomons, who believed that gold coins were imbued with evil spirits, and preferred to be remunerated with six-week courses in teamwork and self-actualization.

You have some people who say, "Our objective is to be the most enlightened work environment in the world." And then you have others who say, "Our objective is to make a lot of money." The value-based people look at the commercial folks as heathens; the commercial people look at the values people as wusses getting in the way.
— Peter Jacobi, president of Levi Strauss & Co., in 1999

aspiration figure, *n.* A must-have doll or action figure. Barbie, originator of the species, began life as a mildly pornographic adult doll named Lilli, discovered in Switzerland in 1959 and subsequently domesticated by Ruth Handler, cofounder of Mattel Inc. The Jack Welch doll, discovered by General Electric in Welch's native Massachusetts in the 1960s, is now available in Casual Friday, Davos summit and Pebble Beach golf-course outfits.

associate, *n.* Flattering title in lieu of a living wage, pioneered by Wal-Mart and other parsimonious employers in the retail trade.

We are men and women, living our lives, doing our share, doing it with dignity, doing it in the most respectable way.
— John Wanamaker, pioneer dry-goods merchant, who refused to have his employees called "shopgirls" or "help." But he made them work Saturdays.

assumed name, *n.* Adopted name that, if successful, betrays no hint of what the company actually does. Initially a means of shedding a stigma. (Standard Oil, of antitrust infamy, became Exxon.) Currently a device for jazzing up stodgy firms, as in Unisys (the merged Sperry Corp. and Burroughs Corp.), Accenture (formerly Anderson Consulting), Vectren (né Indiana Energy) and Venator Group (F. W. Woolworth).

This name could have come out of Star Trek. *Wasn't Vectren a Klingon general?*
— U.S. fund manager Mark Dawson

At Dell/P&G/Harvard/Stanford, we used to …, *phrase.* Career-arresting reference when addressing a superior who is proud of his status as a Harvard dropout (Bill Gates) or who quit a job with P&G flogging Pampers in the Midwest (Steve Case). A better opening gambit for Microgeeks: "One of the amazing, transformational things I learned from reading Bill's *The Road Ahead* was …"

available for reassignment, *adj.* Available for an exit interview. Her mistake was to not drag out her last assignment until she had lined up some new project to prove her indispensability.

b-to-b, *adj.* Originally web-speak for "business-to-business" Internet gear and services. More recently, after the dot-com bust, an acronym for "back to banking," the field many Internet entrepreneurs came from, and to which they are returning. "B-to-c," originally "business-to-consumer" outfits, now means back to consulting.

back story, *n.* Events leading up to the current debacle, hushed up until now. In the aftermath of the CEO's ouster, it is revealed that he faked both his doctorate in zoology and his stint as a Peace Corps worker in Equatorial Guinea. Erstwhile sycophants now recall his poor table manners, weakness for management bestsellers selected by Oprah's book club and a wild karaoke night in Tampa, where he painted whiskers on his face and lip-synched the score of *Cats*.

bad-boy clause, *n.* Employment-contract stipulation that strips a defecting top executive of accrued pension, stock and other benefits if she tries to lure former colleagues to her new employer.

bailiwick, I won't interfere in your, *phrase.* No point helping you look good.

balloon juice, *n.* Extravagant boasting. "I thought I was going to gag when he started giving us that balloon juice about how he'd once brought IBM to its knees."

ball's in your court, The, *phrase.* I've put you in an impossible situation. Now, go along with it, or walk away.

banalysis, *n.* A trite summary with a platitude on top.

Communications technologies are the engines of change and growth in the world's economy at the moment – and that gives us a wealth of opportunities. Our task is to seize those opportunities, deliver excellent value for shareholders and, in doing so, realize our vision of becoming the most successful worldwide telecommunications group.
— Sir Peter Bonfield, CEO of British Telecommunications PLC, in his annual message to shareholders in 1998. Three years later, the debt-burdened BT, no match for its nimble competitors, was broken up.

banana problem, *n.* A problem with a surfeit of possible solutions, inspired by the old saw about how difficult it is to spell "banana" (when do you stop?). For instance, the moribund website that the designers can't stop redesigning after experimenting with 18 perfectly acceptable versions.

banana problem, one-, *n.* A challenge that even a trained monkey could handle. Too bad there's never a trained monkey around when you need one.

banding, *n.* Pecking-order mechanism that arbitrarily determines everything from salary ranges to the size of one's office according to the title an employee holds in the organization. While the office of a mere vice president is outfitted with a modest chesterfield, managers who cross the "tree line" in the corporate hierarchy – senior vice presidents and above – are entitled to three potted trees, a conference table and a painting from the corporate art bank.

bandwidth, *n.* 1. Capacity of a telecommunications network, especially one that carries Internet traffic. 2. Mental capacity, lacking in those without sufficient bandwidth to grasp difficult concepts. 3. Among stressed-out geeks, a reference to time: "I don't have the bandwidth to deal with that right now."

banker, *n.* Enabler of last resort.

If bankers are busy, there is something wrong.
– Walter Bagehot, nineteenth-century British economist and journalist

Time will tell whether I have the qualities for this job. But I've been in banking 27 years, and you can teach a monkey any business after 27 years. After all, it's not brain surgery.
– Matthew Barrett, CEO of Bank of Montreal in the 1990s, and of Barclays PLC, in 2001

bankruptcy, Chapter 11, *n*. Temporary refuge from creditors, in which the full measure of calamity can be assessed with protection from claim seekers. Usually this is a bid to achieve defeat with honor; but some firms actually regain their health and emerge to make a second stab at notoriety. Bankruptcy junkie: TWA drifted in and out of bankruptcy three times before finally being absorbed by another carrier.

Capitalism without bankruptcy is like Christianity without hell.
– Frank Borman, CEO of Eastern Airlines, RIP

bath menu, *n*. At five-star hotels, an offering of butler-dispensed scented oils, bubble bath, massages and other goodies. These will appear on the expense report as "client-presentation support materials."

beachfront property, *n.* In merger transactions, assets of the acquired company that the purchaser wishes to keep. Everything not close to the water's edge is ripe for disposal.

bear hug, *n.* Crushing embrace of a white knight that proposes to rescue a takeover target from its prey by acquiring the target for itself.

bear trap, *n.* A brief surge in stock prices during a longer-term collapse in the market, lasting just long enough to lure foolhardy investors into buying deep-discount stocks that are poised to fall further in value.

bee with a bone, *n.* A person obsessed with an issue vastly larger than himself. For instance, the cafeteria worker at GE who frets that CEO Jack Welch's retirement will trigger a global depression.

beeper pay, *n.* Modest compensation for being constantly on call, meted out in *ad hoc* payments rather than a more gratifying hike in salary.

bennies, *n.* HR talk for employee benefits. These include enriched pensions, health insurance and on-site gourmet-coffee bars for employees who mainline caffeine to sustain their 24/7 workstyles.

Quick – before the HMO is gone – refill the Xanax, Zovirax, Paxil, Vicodin, Claritin, Viagra.
 – Advice on coping with imminent job loss, in *Esquire*, 2001

best-before date (**sell-by date** in the U.K.), *n*. The shelf life of a trend ("Quality circles are so yesterday"), or a product (When was the last time you heard someone admire how good you look in your "Calvins"?), or a person ("Jim's one bright idea made him a visionary for a while, but now he's behind the curve").

best practices, *n*. Consultants' research culled by reading magazine profiles of successful CEOs, then sold to dullard corporate clients with the promise that they too can flourish by emulating these fine examples.

beta tester, *n*. Guinea pig. Volunteer testers are "first movers," eager to be the first victims to work out bugs in their fuel cell-powered car or self-cleaning backyard barbecue. Unwitting testers are supermarket shoppers in demographically correct towns like Peoria, Illinois, who periodically encounter items like calcium-enriched Snickers bars and squab in a tube; and anyone who buys a software package without noticing the label Release 1.0.

big hairy audacious goal (BHAG), *n*. A candidly ridiculous objective with which the CEO hopes to frighten her slow-witted troops into action.

big iron, *n.* Room-sized mainframe computers, IBM's specialty, which crunch numbers at hospitals, airports and insurance factories. Mocked by webheads as relics of computing prehistory, they lack the agility of modern PCs, laptops and handheld computers. The latter, of course, can simultaneously download your household-budget spreadsheet and MP3 music files while monitoring instant-messaging traffic without crashing. Well, don't they?

big room, *n.* Outdoors. The vast space, lit by a big yellow dot in daytime and by tiny white lights at night, that is located outside all computer facilities. "Can he call you back? He's somewhere out in the big room."

bio-break, *n.* A trip to the washroom.

bitstorm, *n.* Borrowed from the computerese for data bits, an overabundance of information that clouds rather than clarifies an issue.

blamestorming, *n.* Fault-finding among co-workers eager to expose someone else as the author of the recent misfortune.

bloatware, *n.* Clunky, memory-consuming software with more features than anyone could ever need. Also refers to the ton of briefing materials that must be studied prior to the meeting.

board bulking, *n.* Recruitment of able directors to strengthen a board that, in a company's start-up phase, was stocked with friends, family and college buddies of the founder. Their company started out as a dorm party. But now they're trying to bulk up on people who know about refinancing, marketing strategy – things that require more smarts than sneaking a goat into the dean's office.

bond in drag, *n.* A sure-and-steady firm whose shares mimic the conservative performance of a bond.

boom mentality, *n.* A euphoric attitude that holds that Newton might have exaggerated the power of gravity.

If you've got Nasdaq stock, it's like having Confederate money.
– Actor Robin Williams on the *Today* show in April 2000, a few days after the big bust in Internet stocks

People are feeling really wounded because they bought stocks at 100 times revenues, and they can't understand why their life's savings is gone. People, get a grip! Look at what you did! Hey, that truck hit me! Well, if you play in the freeway, you are going to get hit by a truck.
– Scott McNealy, CEO of Sun Microsystems Inc., in March 2001, when stock in his own firm was down 72 percent from its all-time high

boomerang, *n.* Return of the corporate native, after the flameout of the Internet start-up to which he recently defected. His disloyalty is usually forgiven since he is easily assimilated (no training required).

booster shot, *n.* "Buy" recommendation for a stock that has swooned soon after its initial sale to the public, administered by the "impartial" research department of the underwriter who first brought the shares to market. Just what the spin doctor ordered.

booth babe, *n.* The siren who lures prospects into the vendors' booths at trade shows.

boss button, *n.* Computer icon that, when clicked, quickly fills the screen with boss-friendly texts under headings such as "20 Ways to Be a More Efficient Employee." The recruiting website for Cisco Systems Inc., the networking firm, helpfully provides a button marked "Oh no! My boss is coming." Job seekers who click the button get a web page with headlines that include "List of Gift Ideas for My Boss and Workmates."

boutique, *n.* Polite term for an undercapitalized, understaffed, shoebox-sized operation that revels in its creativity but must farm out everything from payroll management to small photocopying jobs.

braindump, *n.* Bequest by the departing employee or contractor, who tells his successor all there is to know about how to do the job – an assignment to which the defector generally devotes all of 15 minutes.

brain mint, *n.* A break from work to indulge in fleeting rewards like computer solitaire, checking the notice board for new yoga-class postings and taking a ride down the elevator to see if the lobby's still there.

brainstorming session, *n.* A place to check out ideas that will never fly. Anyone with a truly great idea imparts it only to someone with signing authority.

break the rules, *phrase.* An invitation to become a hero by reaping profits from unorthodox methods, or be eaten alive by the entrenched bureaucracy if your rule-breaking approach proves unsuccessful.

bridging to retirement, *n.* Accelerated qualification for full-pension eligibility by firms eager to shed workers of a certain age. After treating you like a potentially rebellious teenager all these years, with its conformist rules and traditions, suddenly the firm wants to think of you as a 65-year-old.

burn rate, *n.* Pace at which a start-up firm incinerates its start-up funds. Typically the conflagration doesn't get out of control until after the initial public offering of its shares.

It's okay to have a company fail, and to start again. At least it is in Silicon Valley. Sometimes you don't even have to change the place where you park your car.
– Venture capitalist John Doerr of California-based Kleiner Perkins Caufield and Byers

burping the elephant, *n.* The expulsion by a mammoth enterprise of an underperforming asset of negligible size as with GM's decision to wind down its Oldsmobile division.

buyer's strike, *n.* Righteous fasting by purchasing officers, whose indignation is in comic contrast to their frenzied order-placing just before the economy dived.

buy-in, *n.* The embrace by employees of an idea proposed by management, who are said to have taken "ownership" of it. Which means the employees must figure out how to make it work, while managers figure out how they will deploy the proceeds of their enhanced share options if the employees succeed in the endeavor.

buyout, *n.* A good-natured inducement for the employee to stop taking up space at the company, best acted upon to avoid the less gracious kiss-off that awaits resisters.

buzz cycle, *n.* A verbal chain letter. Managers of a wannabe hot stock, Acme Networks Co., pass along the good news about Acme's glowing prospects to a stock underwriter hoping to profit from an initial offering of Acme's stock. The underwriter plants a bug about Acme in the ear of its securities analysts, whose pay is tied to underwriting profits. The analysts then tip media touts in search of a scoop to the unheralded promise of Acme's networks. The media stock mavens, in turn, broadcast the good news about Acme to investors glued to CNBC while working out on their rowing machines, who talk up Acme back at the office. Pretty soon everyone owns stock in a company with a market cap of $47 billion founded two months ago by a pair of 23-year-olds in their parents' garage.

C

capital preservation, *n.* 1. At the point of maximum fear, the company elects to hoard cash rather than invest in its future. 2. At the point of maximum safety, the saver opts for the mattress as a substitute for outside-world speculations.

career transition program, *n.* A generous offer to instruct the layoff victim in résumé preparation techniques.

cash positive, *adj.* More money coming in than going out. The executive bonuses are safe.

casual Friday, *n.* Conspiracy by Gap, Eddie Bauer and Dockers to steal market share from Brooks Brothers. And a nightmare for men who once could get away with wearing the same suit to the office every day for 14 years.

Our dress code is, you must dress.
  – Scott McNealy, CEO of Sun Microsystems Inc.

casual Friday, extreme, *n.* An invitation by cost-cutting firms to take Fridays off as unpaid vacation.

catch-and-release program, *n.* Abrupt layoffs at the once fast-growing company that has burned through its cash, just months after the firm swept new recruits off their feet at college job fairs.

chair plug, *n.* Innocuous space-filler at meetings and conferences. "Oh, was Bill there? Where was he sitting, exactly?"

chairman emeritus, *n.* Tribal mystic, a living reminder of the golden days before the business got complicated. His charming nostrums lack authority (he no longer has power) but not authenticity (he once was God).

challenge, *n.* Euphemism for danger ahead. The company that acknowledges it faces "a challenging period" is admitting that it (a) is in big trouble, and (b) isn't quite sure what to do about it. Bet on this company as you would on someone preparing to swim blindfolded through an alligator pond.

change agent, *n.* Self-styled revolutionary who proposes swapping old dysfunctionalities for new ones.

character-building project, *n*. A scheme that is doomed to fail. In traditional corporate life, casualties of such fiascoes are shuffled off to "special projects," the bureaucratic equivalent of Siberia. In Silicon Valley, Don Quixotes who pursue flaky ideas are rewarded with venture capital funding.

I can tolerate one or two mistakes, then I'll cut their hearts out with a spoon.
 – Katherine Hammer, CEO of Evolutionary Technologies International, on dealings with her research scientists

character loan, *n*. Funds extended to a prudent borrower who splurges every few years on a new suit from Sears, has never appeared in the society pages and has not acquired a trophy spouse – who is not, in fact, a "character."

chief table pounder, *n*. The most prominently relentless champion of a new way of doing things, often accused of Elmer Gantry excesses.

chipmunking, *n*. In meetings, the pose of the furtive hand-held-device user, who is scrunched up, elbows extended, arms close to the chest, fingers rapidly tapping out a message to an unseen correspondent. "They look like they're working on a little nut or something," says Hugh Martin, chief executive at ONI Systems, a San Jose, California, fiber-optic company.

"I get their attention by telling them: 'You're chipmunking!' I mean, don't they look like a chipmunk?"

circling the drain, *n*. Slipping away. A time for frenzied but futile last efforts to save a doomed project or enterprise.

class-action lawsuit, *n*. A pity party of aggrieved souls who should have known better than to live near the polluting factory, buy the bargain-priced defective tires, medicate themselves with the inefficacious baldness cure and invest in the overhyped shares.

cockroach theory, *n*. The first outbreak of bad news will not be the last.

It's such a negative environment everybody believes in the cockroach theory right now – if you see one profit warning you're going to see more.
– Wachovia Securities analyst George Hunt, in 2001

code brown, *n*. A rapidly deteriorating situation. Inspired by the hospital term for a spell of bowel incontinence that can be detected throughout the ward. "Stay away from the Gemstar project. Their budget's frozen, staffing's been cut – the whole thing is code brown."

code of conduct, *n.* Guidebook that enumerates unacceptable behavior and identifies by omission antisocial acts that may still be safely committed.

coffin kick, *n.* Running commentary by media ghouls on the mounting failure rate in a given industry sector, under cute labels like "Net.Bombs" and "Dot-com Deathwatch," compiled by journalists who've never met a payroll and couldn't run a two-car funeral.

commune, *n.* A company where everyone, and therefore no one, is in charge. Tip-offs: Beaded curtains for walls, rotating potluck luncheon assignments and the in-house psychologist is acting CEO on Tuesdays.

company states, *n.* Alarmists' term for global leviathans such as IBM, ExxonMobil and Ford, whose revenues and unique customs match the GNP and cumbersome bureaucracy of many large countries.

compensation committee, *n.* A club within a club, the cozy knot of directors who determine CEO pay. They try not to be influenced by the fact that they owe their $100,000-a-year board seat to an ability to get along with the CEO whom they are ostensibly supervising, and that they count on the CEO's firm to spend lavishly on services provided by the law, brokerage, accounting and other supplier firms where they are employed in their day jobs.

compensation, executive, *n*. Salary, bonus, options and perks secured by CEOs and other top officers in an open-auction process that results in pay packets that would make Croesus blush.

It didn't make a hell of a lot of difference if the guy had just screwed up or invented LEXAN [a lucrative General Electric plastic]. It was just unreal. You'd take the size of the guy's shirt collar and divide it by the Gregorian calendar and multiply it by the square root of pi, and you'd come out with a number that was totally meaningless.
– Walter Wriston, former CEO of Citibank and a director of GE, on how GE once determined pay packages for top executives

competitive intelligence, *n*. Corporate espionage conducted by surprisingly old-fashioned snoops. Posing as prospective customers or as journalists, these spies pluck a company's clients, suppliers and former and existing employees clean of sensitive information using the time-tested devices of plausibility, flattery, congeniality and flirtation.

When a client wants to find out information, what you are doing on their behalf is in effect a sophisticated form of mystery shopping.
  – Michael Herson, director of Britain's Strategy Works, a firm of data gumshoes

compliance event, *n.* An outbreak of lawlessness at the firm, which it chooses to describe as noncompliance to distinguish the befouling of Prince William Sound from a routine milkstore holdup.

computer literacy, *n.* Term used by the computer industry to convince users that they are to blame in failing to master machines and software that, in fact, are not "human literate."

conference lag, *n.* Exhausting ritual of catching up on work missed while enduring the New Paradigms in Customer-Driven Success summit.

conglomerate, *n.* An extended family of subsidiaries that squabble over allowances and pursue careers that conflict with each other.

consensus builder, *n.* One who appears able to keep the group out of trouble.

consoltant, *n.* A grief counselor who attends to employees designated for layoff.

constituency, *n.* Any group you care about, including big-spending customers, motivated employees, loyal suppliers and major shareholders who could make trouble with the board. Everyone else is rabble.

constructive dismissal, *n.* Staged removal of an employee who is handed a succession of unpleasant, impossible tasks and accumulates a record of failure that legally justifies his ultimate firing.

consultant, *n.* A passing stranger paid to visit your home and criticize the decor, making suggested improvements she will not have to live with.

I have my Andy Warhol theory of management concepts. What is hot now will be colder than a wet dog in six months.
– Management consultant David Bratton on the durability of empowerment, total quality management and other workplace fads

consulting, I have real freedom now that I'm, *phrase.* I have freedom now that I'm between real jobs. And I have real headaches from being my own benefits administrator.

content provider, *n.* Maker of movies, sitcoms, music, books, magazines or newspapers, whose output is stuffed into "pipelines" or "distribution channels" – that is, your mailbox or TV set.

context, *n.* Not what was said, but by whom, and where and when, and in whose presence. And has he or she been heard from since?

continuous improvement, *n.* A conviction that everything can be done faster and cheaper, with fewer employees and at a higher profit margin. Perfected in the 1980s by Japanese automakers and regarded by American industry as a second Pearl Harbor until U.S. firms learned how to emulate it.

convergence, *n.* 1. Investment banking scheme for generating merger and acquisition fees by counseling media moguls to assemble unwieldy empires that combine the means of production ("content providers" such as the producer of *Ally McBeal* and the publisher of *Sports Illustrated*) with the means of distribution (TV networks, cable companies, movie-house chains). As yet, there are no paying customers for this proposition. 2. Investment banking scheme for generating merger and acquisition fees by counseling telecommunications firms to accumulate massive debts in constructing upgraded networks capable of transmitting phone, Internet, cable and other signals over the same wire. Not quite all of the paying customers for this proposition have filed for Chapter 11 bankruptcy protection.

cookie-jar accounting, *n.* Cash reserves set aside for dipping into when flagging profits need a boost, obscuring the true condition of the income statement.

cordial compulsion campaign, *n.* Process by which companies propel employees into early retirement with onetime bonuses and sweetened pension plans.

core competency, *n.* The one thing you are, or were, really good at. Which is sadly disguised by the boondoggles that your one brush with competence gave you the confidence to pursue.

corporate reputation management, *n.* Public relations. A routine function that can be handled with press releases until a factory explodes, at which point it becomes necessary to refocus public attention on all the factories that have not exploded.

corporate social responsibility, *n.* A self-congratulatory exercise in obeying various laws applying to employment equity, environmental protection, safe workplaces and the like without having to be prodded into compliance by regulators.

Good friends, good books and a sleepy conscience. This is the ideal life.
– Mark Twain

correction, inventory-led, *n.* An economic slowdown triggered by a lapse in judgment among producers, who are corrected in imagining that there was an inexhaustible demand for their wares.

corrective intervention, *n.* The recruitment of an outsider, often a human resources consultant, to broker peace among warring office politicians whose conflict threatens to destroy the enterprise.

cost, sunk, *n.* Irretrievably spent, beyond the reclamation of all but the bankruptcy court.

couch potato strategy, *n.* A decision to invest in a stock market index fund rather than think for yourself. It is based on the theory that the market fluctuations resulting from the multitude of mistakes made by other investors each day represent an improvement over your own localized mischief in detecting a buying opportunity in Sears, Roebuck stock when you couldn't find a parking spot there last weekend.

cow chip, *n.* A former blue-chip company, transformed, as in Johns-Manville, A. H. Robins, Xerox and Lucent Technologies, into a fiscal basket case by market share reversals, debt-related illiquidity or class-action litigation.

creatively negative, *adj.* The CEO's behavior in revealing every scrap of bad news that has been accumulating at her firm, timed for an industrywide downturn that will hopefully obscure her own torrent of pent-up disclosures.

creepback, *n.* Reappearance of laid-off employees as part-time workers and "contractors" after a staff purge that has removed essential employees along with deadwood. After repeated downsizings in the 1980s and 1990s, creepback at GM, Kodak, IBM and other employers meant that their payroll levels were little changed by 2001.

crisis management, *n.* 1. Process of fixing what went wrong, apologizing for it and making sure it can't happen again – an exercise that in Japan achieves closure with the dignified resignation of a CEO who accepts responsibility and blame. 2. Process of fixing the blame, always as low in the ranks as possible, to ensure "plausible deniability" for the CEO and other higher-ups; and of faulting critics for making allegations based on data that is necessarily incomplete, given that someone is busy feeding it into a shredder.

cross-sell, *v.* Get the customer to also buy one of your other fine products. "You know what goes great with car mats, sir? Deck stain!" "While I'm updating your savings account passbook, madam, I wonder if you'd give some thought to hedging your mortgage obligations using yen-backed subordinated debentures issued by Royal Dutch/Shell?"

"C" title, *n.* A tag that signals changing priorities at the firm, vesting authority in formerly uncelebrated satraps such as the chief financial officer (the ranking bean counter), the chief information/technology officer (IT paymaster), the chief talent officer (in-house headhunter), the chief strategy officer (top compass reader), the chief morale officer (editor of the in-house newsletter) and the chief environment officer (lobbyist who pushes for company-friendly eco-regulations).

cube counter, *n.* Hatchet-person who, with geometric precision, executes orders to eliminate 20 cubicle people per hundred cubicles a workplace where a 20 percent "headcount reduction" has been targeted.

cube farm, *n.* A warren of isolation cells offering less room than prisoners are afforded in maximum stir.

cubicle creativity, *n.* Argument for open-office layouts in order to empower the rank and file, holding that the physical confines of a drone's workspace put a similar constraint on her brainpower. "Most people experience cubicle creativity," said Gerald Haman, a U.S. consultant on stimulating innovative thinking in bureaucratic organizations. "The size of their ideas is directly proportional to the space they have in which to think."

cubicle lizard, *n.* Pasty-faced colleague rumored never to have stepped off the premises, and hunkered down in a workspace outfitted with creature comforts. The shaving mirror, microwave oven and library of Nintendo CDs are giveaways that this is not your co-worker's *second* home.

cubicle people, *n.* Clock-watchers who resent their role as anonymous cogs in a soulless organization, but not enough to face the world without a drug plan.

cuddle factor, *n.* Marketing gambit to dress up technology as cute, user-friendly and nostalgic, as in Pokémon, the iMac computer, the new VW Beetle and the PT Cruiser.

customer comes first, The, *phrase.* That's why we call them end users.

Hierarchy is an organization with its face toward the CEO, and its ass toward the customer. Pleasing the boss should never be more important than pleasing the customer.
– Jack Welch, CEO of General Electric

customer-driven, *adj.* Inspired by the customer's insistence that the product be reliable, safe, multifunctional, cheap, powerful, compatible, user-friendly, cheap, readily available, fully guaranteed, service-supported and *cheap* – no matter how much the yoinks in the focus groups said they'd be willing to pay for it.

customer-initiated communication, *n*. A call to the complaints department.

customer intimacy, *n*. A caring, empathetic regard for the client, based on shared values and aspirations. Just kidding. The use of intimate details about the customer's shopping habits to drain her pockets on a more or less continual basis.

customer satisfaction, *n*. What the market will bear.

I asked a psychologist recently why he thought people react so violently to service charges, and he said maybe they're feeling like somebody who has just been charged for breakfast by their mother.
 – Matthew Barrett, CEO of Barclays PLC

Let's see, we've gone from "meeting customer expectations," to "exceeding customer expectations," to "delighting customers," to "customer ecstasy." I hate to see what's next.
 – Len Schlesinger, executive vice president at U.S. retailer The Limited Inc.

customer service, *n*. What the client will endure.

All you have to do to run a cable TV company is get a license from the city and be mean to your customers.
 – U.S. mutual fund manager Ralph Wanger

As long as customers are born faster than we can make them hate us, we're in business.

– A U.S. airline ticket agent describes the relationship between passengers and airline personnel in a 2001 report in the *New York Times*

cyber-pseud, *n.* "If Gates had any sense he'd stymie Justice by net-backing Oracle's Paradigm III suite – which rocks, by the way – and use that as a platform architecture to build a whole new operating environment – yes, I will have a canapé."

cyberspace, *n.* A consensual hallucination about the ethereal realm where virtual profits will someday be harvested from products and services made possible by virtual technology, all sight unseen.

daddy track, *n.* Career route of the man who sacrifices his shot at promotion by spending inordinate time with his offspring. A fiction created by men's rights groups that insist the "mommy track" is a myth, citing as evidence the appearance of four female CEOs on the Fortune 500 – a 300 percent increase in recent years!

data dump, *n.* Management's habit of preparing directors for board meetings by asking them to digest a stack of impenetrable documents when seeking their approval in a crucial decision.

data mining, *n.* Covert accumulation of personal data on clients, often gleaned from credit card records, to stimulate the spendthrift habits of repeat customers.

data point, soft, *n.* Suggestive but not firm evidence. Data based on anecdotes, gossip, inference and speculation.

When Aunt Midge starts serving tenderloin again, it's time to go long on cattle futures.

data sponge, *n.* Superabsorbent manager whose data-sogged brain has been rendered useless for other activity. "If he wasn't such a data sponge we'd have a decision by now."

day trading, *n.* Obsessive equity trading by credulous fortune seekers who divine the future from a glowing computer screen in the den. Formerly these people could be seen at the beach poking about with a metal detector.

dead cat bounce, *n.* A brief, unconvincing recovery in a battered stock. A stock that's hitting bottom may bounce a few times, but there's no life in it. Also known as a "feline uptick."

If you drop a dead cat off a tall enough building, he's going to bounce.
– U.S. money manager Binkley Shorts of the Over-The-Counter Securities Fund

dead money, *n.* An investment whose value hasn't budged since the pyramids were built.

Only dead fish swim with the current.
– Mark Mobius, mutual fund manager

death march, *n.* Parade of 25-hour days leading up to the deadline for a new-product launch. An echo of Napoleon's assault on Russia, except that his troops were better fed than the pizza-fueled laborers in Silicon Valley.

In five years we will realize that the dot-coms, with their 70-hour weeks, Nerf balls, and self-consciously zany atmosphere, damaged the work ethic in more ways than we can imagine. The attempt to con people into working longer hours by making the workplace "fun" is an empty cheat.
– Rob Lawrence in *Forbes ASAP*, in 2001

de-layering, *n.* The decision to save money by shedding a protective covering of middle managers – an unwelcome opportunity for top management to rub shoulders with the rank and file.

delegate, *v.* To empower subordinates by sticking them with tasks from which you derive no enjoyment or glory.

Has anyone given you the law of these offices? No? It is this. Nobody does anything if he can get anybody else to do it. As soon as you can, get someone whom you can rely on, train him in the work, sit down, cock up your heels, and think out some way for Standard Oil to make some money.
– John D. Rockefeller

deliverable, *n.* 1. A product or service that results from the R&D, marketing and manufacturing process, now on sale at Kmart. 2. An earthshaking document yielded by a seminar, off-site retreat, high-level summit, facilitator-led encounter session or bull-pit confrontation with the CEO. The CEO will implement the resulting policy paper after confirming that it jibes with the hunch she started out with.

denial, *n.* If you can keep your head when all about you are losing theirs, possibly you have no idea what trouble you're in.

de-skilling, *n.* The process by which a worker's previously coveted skills are rendered useless by new technology. Or by the arrival of a new CEO, whose political strategies mystify her new peers.

desk potato, *n.* Semi-invalid whose physical exertions are limited to cradling a phone, cleaning lint from the computer keyboard and experimenting with new colors of Post-it notes.

development stage company, *n.* A concept that boasts no visible means of support other than its stock market listing.

digital campfire, *n.* Computer workstations formed in a circle for intimate collegiality – and for keeping an eye on potential slackers.

digitalia, *n*. Indispensable gadgets of the wired world – your PC, notebook, wireless e-mail receiver, PDA, cell phone, wrist-top device and all the other miniaturized circuitry that makes you an overconnected node in the global town square.

director, *n*. They also serve who silently witness the gathering storm and then nod off.

How mistaken I have been in dividing myself among so many activities, and how foolish my vanity has been in leading me to occupy positions which I filled with but little real quality or excellence.
 – Sir Joseph Flavelle, Canadian industrialist and promiscuous corporate director, in 1903

The pleasant but vacuous director need never worry about job security.
 – Warren Buffett

director, non-executive, n. A board member who is not a full-time officer of the company and literally phones in some of her infrequent contributions.

dirt in the oyster, *n*. A catalyst for change, whose insistent and irritating calls for innovation might someday give birth to a lucrative new line of business.

disambiguate, *v.* Clarify, make clear.

You've got to take the bull between your teeth.
– Movie mogul Samuel Goldwyn

discontinuity, *n.* An apparent disruption in the market, said to arise from complex demographic and technological "dislocations" and other ephemera. A handy term for excusing the complacency by which a firm has allowed itself to lose ground to a competing product that is vaguely similar to what it offers, only better and cheaper.

disengaged, actively, *adj.* Term for employees who complain they don't know what's expected of them, lack the materials to do their jobs and aren't able to get the attention of their bosses. As opposed to passive malcontents, who also don't like their jobs but aren't sure why.

disintermediation, *n.* A term for "cutting out the middleman" that doesn't economize on syllables.

doctor's appointment, *n.* Off-site job interview. Then again, maybe Kevin traded dungarees for a suit today because he likes to look his best for blood tests.

dog food, *n.* Software not fit for external consumption but adequate for use by the programmers who wrote it.

domestic, *n.* A dispute between colleagues that gives co-workers the idea that in a previous life the combatants must have been married.

doom loop, *n.* Bold but undisciplined steps taken by the incoming leader who is bent on making a decisive impression, the failure of which triggers still more chaos as corrective maneuvers are attempted.

dotted-line relationship, *n.* Ill-defined connection by which a shadowy adviser who does not report to the boss has her ear just the same. Usually held by a person with no tangible responsibilities, but who is generous with criticism of those who do.

download, *v.* Originally the use of a computer to access data from another computer, now referring to the retrieval of all things from machines and people alike. "Jim was no help when I was downloading Stan about how his meeting went with Kendall. He just parked himself in front of the vending machine, downloading Clark bars."

downsizing, *n.* A decision to spare employees the misery of enduring any further bungles of top management by relieving them of their jobs. The term originated in the 1970s with the "down-sizing" of automobiles by Motown, and has applied to surplus employees since the early 1980s.

The business world has more expressions for downsizing than Eskimos do for snow. Among them are bright-sizing, building-down, census reduction, compressing, chemistry change, career assessment, decruitment, de-growing, de-hiring, de-selecting, de-staffing, de-massing, downshifting, executive culling, five-alarm firings, force reduction, headcount reduction, human capital re-engineering, imbalance correction, indefinite idling, involuntary separation, leaning up, management-initiated attrition, natural wastage, organizational redesign, personnel surplus reduction, redeployment, rationalizing, redundancy elimination, right-sizing, selecting out, selective separation, skill-mix adjustment, smart-sizing, transitioning, and workforce realignment. Also "betrayal" – a reference to the unwritten social contract that once existed between lifetime employees and the enterprises to which they cheerlessly conformed.

A company that bets its future on its people must remove that lower 10%, and keep removing it every year – always raising the bar of performance and increasing the quality of its leadership.
– Jack Welch, CEO of General Electric

dribbleware, *n.* Software released in tiny increments, enabling the vendor to fatten its total profits, as with encyclopedias sold by volume rather than set.

drill down, *v.* Get at the root of things. As with oil exploration, a costly and laborious activity undertaken only with prior assurance that riches lurk below. "I'm not going to drill down on this until I find out if Bob's previous ideas have led to anything."

driver, *n.* Motive force. The market demand that is driving the popularity of a product. The product that is driving the profits of the company. The heroic executive who is driving the lucrative product.

drool factor, *n.* Attractiveness of a takeover target, evident from the large number of potential buyers who can't hide their covetous regard for it.

drop-dead date, *n.* Absolute final deadline, give or take a few weeks.

dumbsizing, *n.* Sweeping layoffs that oust valued employees along with idlers, leaving the employer ill prepared for the next upturn.

dynamic, *n.* A catchall rubric for the conditions that apply, suggesting unmanageable volatility. A fancy term meant to excuse one's lack of control over events. "It's a curious dynamic: People see a better, cheaper product, and they buy that one instead of ours."

E

early stage investment, *n.* A bet placed on a fledgling company whose founders only recently achieved the status of no longer requiring their parents' signatures on legal documents.

earnings, managed, *n.* The financial statement as a work of historical fiction. Anticipated revenues are booked as current ones. Current expenses are represented as future ones. And budgets for advertising, capital expenditures, employee training and the like are "adjusted" up or down so that the company is able to report profits that precisely match the forecasts it earlier made to Wall Street analysts. The awestruck analysts understate matters in commending management for having such an intimate knowledge of the business.

If the profit numbers on income statements are treated with such reverence, it was obviously only a question of time before some smart

fellows would start building companies not around the logical progression of a business but around what would beef up the numbers.
— Adam Smith, *The Money Game* (1967)

The figure to watch is cash flow. You can only fake cash flow if you are willing to risk going to jail. Earnings are a less accurate indicator. It takes very little to change an earnings picture completely.
— Management guru Peter Drucker

EBITDA, *n.* Earnings before interest, taxes, depreciation and amortization — a new method for depicting profit that is designed to flatter the CEO. Its accuracy holds for a wide universe of companies, except those that carry debt, pay taxes and have assets that depreciate.

Of the 147 companies tracked by Moody's Investor Services that defaulted on their debt last year, most borrowed money based on EBITDA performance. I'll bet the bankers in those deals wish they'd looked at a few other factors.
— Herb Greenberg in *Fortune*, in 2000

References to EBITDA make us shudder — does management think the tooth fairy pays for capital expenditures?
— Warren Buffett, letter to shareholders of Berkshire Hathaway Inc., in 2001

economic cycle, *n.* A phenomenon as enduring as the biblical 7 years of feasting and subsequent 7 years of famine. Rumors of its abolition are a sure sign that times of exhilarating prosperity are about to end.

We compulsively associate unusual intelligence with the leadership of great financial institutions, even though for practical purposes, the financial memory should be assumed to last, at a maximum, no more than 20 years. This is normally the time it takes for the recollection of one disaster to be erased and for some variant on previous dementia to come forward to capture the financial mind.
 – John Kenneth Galbraith

edifice complex, *n.* The corporate naming-rights trend that has given us sporting venues with quaint monikers like PacBell Park, HSBC Arena and PSINet Stadium.

ego surfing, *n.* Searching for one's own name on the Internet and in other media.

electrons, Tidying up the, *phrase.* Clearing the backlog of e-mail messages.

elevator music, *n.* Comforting assertions of higher corporate purpose, including the annual report and the firm's vision, values and mission statements. All are seized upon by outside observers for signs of inconsistency between noble intent and sordid practice.

elevator test, *n.* The axiom that the only strategy worth pursuing is one that's simple enough to explain during an elevator ride.

Elisha Gray award, *n.* Consolation prize for runners-up in contests for employees who come up with brainwaves for saving money. Named for the inventor who submitted a patent for the telephone just hours after Alexander Graham Bell.

Elvis year, *n.* Peak moment of a fad's impact. For instance, the second decade of the twentieth century for Henry Ford's Model T, the year 1993 for Barney the purple dinosaur and half an hour in 1985 for the New Coke.

emotional economy, *n.* As distinct from the real economy, popular perceptions and expectations about future economic performance. The emotional economy is fundamentally sound, for instance, when consumers keep maxing out their credit cards even as corporate profits and stock prices are nose-diving.

empathetic disengagement, *n.* Switching customers from tellers to ATMs without alienating them – for instance, by charging them $20 to talk to a real person rather than getting rid of tellers altogether.

employee-involvement program, *n.* The suggestion box.

employee recognition, *n.* Traditionally, a Christmas turkey for everyone on the payroll. More recently, stock options, which, with luck, might someday be cashed in to buy a Christmas turkey.

employment agency, *n.* A company with a bloated payroll that values lifetime employment over efficiency, in which such institutions as General Motors, Siemens and the Japanese banking industry suffer by comparison with the post office.

empowerment, *n.* Responsibility without authority, an invitation to share management's enthusiasm but not the bonus pool.

If you empower dummies, you get bad decisions faster.
 – Rich Teerlink, CEO of Harley-Davidson, on the downside of new management theories

end user, *n.* The customer, who gets it in the end.

end-user experience, *n.* This is nothing like how it was described to me by the salesperson/catalog/website/trade-show rep/celebrity endorser/guy in the next cubicle/sister-in-law at the cottage last summer.

energy drainer, *n.* A worrywart.

Energy drainers are worriers who have more shadows than sunshine. You talk to these people and you feel drained at the end of the conversation. By contrast, energy suppliers don't have all the answers but they say, "Leave it to me, I'll find a way." You feel good being around them and you want more of them.
– Raj Jaswa, founder and CEO of Selectica, a San Jose, California, software firm

enterprise environment, *n.* The office.

entrenched, *adj.* A term for top managers who are past their prime but dug in for a fight against predators poised to inflict their own follies on the company.

equivalent position, *n.* A demotion or sideways move into alien territory that has the intended effect of prompting the resignation of the employee to whom it is offered.

error in judgment, *n.* A high-level blunder that could not be covered up. In the event, the CEO regrets that subordinates have made mistakes in their zeal to act upon his error in judgment.

Worse than a crime; it was a mistake.
– Joseph Fouche, one of Napoleon's ministers

essentials, We need to focus on, *phrase*. We need a detailed breakdown of your daily workflow to confirm our suspicion that what little you do can easily be outsourced.

execution, *n*. Vision with its sleeves rolled up, spitting on both hands.

We don't need any more bright ideas. In business, success is 5 percent strategy, 95 percent execution.
– Peter Banevik, chairman of Swiss-Swedish engineering firm ABB Asea Brown Boveri

exit interview, *n*. Stilted discussion in which the departing employee offers tepid criticisms that the interviewer pretends to absorb while running down a mental checklist of the property and security codes the defector is required to surrender.

exit strategy, *n*. Optimistic plan for cashing in when the venture proves successful. Or the fallback plan if everything goes wrong. Both involve a dacha in a tropical tax haven.

extreme-value retailer, *n*. The everything-for-a-dollar store.

eye candy, *n*. Seductive packaging. Inspired by "ear candy" (c. late 1980s), for platitudes to calm a restless audience.

F

face time, *n.* 1. Personal contact as a last resort when instant messaging fails. 2. A bid for ubiquity by ladder climbers who seek proximity with their presumed betters.

false enthusiasm purchase, *n.* Guilt-induced acquisitions of seldom-used items such as rowing machines, cross-country skis, herbal remedies and Suze Orman's *Guide to Spending and Saving Wisely*.

FAQ, *n.* Frequently asked question. Bane of tech support staff, of whom the most FAQ is, "Where *are* the IT people?"

fashion forward, *adj.* A startling departure from the norm. And ill-fated, not because it is ugly, impractical and available only in colors that do not appear in nature, but because the uneducated consumer is too timid to embrace it.

fast followers, *n.* Companies such as Microsoft and AOL that have a genius for commercializing the innovations of others.

feedback loop, *n.* The CEO solicits feedback from division heads, who tap the knowledge of middle-management advisory teams, which liaise with worker councils, whose ideas so impress the CEO that he has them sewn into a "community quilt" that is installed in the lobby six months prior to the next round of headcount reductions.

feeling issue, *n.* A minor emotional dislocation. For instance, the unease that arises from being left off an e-mail routing list – a cause for minor upset compared with the *grand mal* angst over being cut from the bonus pool.

firewall, *n.* 1. Software that protects the company's IT systems from corruption by hackers. 2. Corkboard where the layoff notices are posted during successive waves of restructuring.

firing, strategic, *n.* Dismissal of an employee before his or her stock options can vest.

first movers, *n.* Self-selected guinea pigs eager to pony up huge sums to be the first to own a new product in its most primitive, cumbersome and bug-ridden form.

fiscally disciplined, *adj*. A firm that has gotten religion about the need to stop burning cash indiscriminately, now that the company has burned down.

flight risk, *n*. 1. Talented employee known to be pursued by, or in pursuit of, headhunters for rival firms. 2. Executive with increasingly itchy feet as internal snoops follow the paper trail that traces the arc of his botched endeavor.

flight to safety, *n*. Lemming-like defection of investors from former growth stocks that are poised to collapse and into staid blue-chip stocks, money market funds and other lower-risk investments.

Depend on the rabbit's foot if you will, but remember it didn't work for the rabbit.
  – R. E. Shay

flush rate, *n*. Money flushed down the rathole on feckless adventures.

foam the runway, *n*. Banker's term for lines of credit hastily arranged prior to the crash landing of a corporate client that has burned through its cash and needs emergency refinancing.

focus group, *n.* Strangers lured off the street who, in exchange for free coffee and muffins, cast a verdict on products they haven't heard of and would never use. A handy scapegoat for failure. Focus groups pronounced favorably on the Edsel and the New Coke.

food, flat, *n.* Comestibles from the vending machine that can be slipped under the door of a colleague on deadline.

footprint, *n.* Market share. The amount of "space" a product occupies in its given category. As the philosopher might have said, a journey to a thousand burger franchises starts with a single toehold. And then suddenly there's a McDonald's on every corner.

force multiplier, *n.* Aide-de-camp who makes his boss more effective by giving her ideas the force of conviction as he projects them in the wider executive ranks. Close cousin of "enabler," who whispers in the greyhound's ear but doesn't follow him to the racetrack.

forecast, economic, *n.* A brave assertion of little value in itself, but useful in comparison with other prognostications in determining a consensus opinion against which one might safely bet.

Forecasts may tell you a great deal about the forecaster; they tell you nothing about the future.
  – Warren Buffett, CEO of Berkshire Hathaway Inc.

I've driven through my share of rainstorms, listening to some radio announcer in a windowless room telling me that it's a sunny day. During a change in economic climate, the biggest mistake a leader can make is not to recognize it. Accurately assessing the business cycle is key to your company's success. Recognize when the weather is shifting. Rain or shine – look out.
  – Walter Wriston, CEO of Citibank from 1967 to 1984

forward-looking statements, *n.* As defined by securities regulators, assertions in a prospectus, press release or other corporate document that wander into the realm of hopeful speculation rather than assured fact, and must be labeled as such to warn investors. Example: "Among the factors that might cause actual results to differ from those indicated by forward-looking statements in this document are sloth in developing new products, myopia in failing to realize that said products have been targeted at the wrong market, a previously undetected competence and zeal among our competitors, and acts of God or the CEO that are inconsistent with sound business practices and attract the attention of class-action litigators."

free agent, *n.* A solo careerist who names her price – stock options, autonomy, a creative and harmonious workplace – and moves on if she doesn't get it. Daniel H. Pink, author of *Free Agent Nation* (2001), says the essential institutions of free agency are Kinko's, Starbucks, Barnes & Noble, Alliance Business Centers, the Internet, Staples, Mall Boxes Etc. and Federal Express. "At Starbucks you buy coffee and get the office free."

freelancer, *n.* Akin to the politician who breaks with the party line, a subordinate executive who makes policy apparently at odds with the CEO's vision. Not necessarily a career-eliminating move if the offender is testing reaction to ideas that excite but cannot yet be associated with the CEO. "Mac wouldn't wander off the reservation like that unless front office wanted to see if there might actually be some buy-in for these batty schemes."

fumigation, *n.* Selective removal of problematic personnel, such as a union organizer on the shop floor, the lowest-grossing salesperson at the dealership, a scheming CEO heir presumptive in the executive suite.

functionality, *n.* All the many things it can do, when it's working properly.

gadget trance, *n.* Obsession with a new tech toy, which for days monopolizes the attention of its gleeful owner and of passersby who must listen to him rave about it.

Gaplash, *n.* Anti-khaki backlash against casual-Friday wear.

gating, *n.* The torturous progress of a new idea through successive stages of approval, or "gates," as it makes its way up the executive hierarchy.

gazelle, *n.* In corporate finance, an agile start-up company with moxie that might just overcome its shortage of capital and management smarts.

geek beacon, *n.* An oversized, digital wristwatch, capable of receiving signals from orbiting satellites and the takeout window at Jack-in-the-Box.

geek chorus, *n.* Passel of techno-solons that urges overworked corporate IT staffs to scrap their (costly) computer infrastructure for new (more costly) gear or risk being left behind as rival buyers clog the vendors' order books.

geeked, *adj.* Wired, strung-out, psyched-up. Tune in, turn on, boot up.

gene jockey, *n.* A financier at a biotech start-up.

gesture tactic, *n.* A feigned interest in employment equity, workplace safety, environmental protection, charitable contributions and other hot-button issues, which begins and ends with rhetoric printed in colorful brochures. A decision to include in the annual report the name of every single employee in lieu of a pay hike.

What we don't like, what we're bound not to like, are the politics of gesture, or the politics of spin, which are not relevant to the company. The issues you can create measurable targets for are generally easier to deal with.
– Sir John Browne, CEO of BP Amoco PLC, on the firm's partnerships with the Environmental Defense advocacy group, the World Wildlife Fund in Bolivia and China, with Oxfam in Angola and with Save the Children in Vietnam

get big fast, *phrase.* Creed of the Internet start-up. Lavish spending by newbie Internet firms on staffing, equipment and marketing, with scant concern for fundamentals such as cost control, profit margins and liquidity soon gave rise to a new saying: How do you launch a small Internet firm? Ramp up a big one, and wait.

global effectiveness, We must strengthen our, *phrase.* We need a longer-range corporate jet. You can't get around the world on a scooter.

global fix, *n.* 1. Programmer's trick for correcting a recurring error, turning all the commas in a spreadsheet program to semicolons. 2. CEO's mind-meld trick for correcting a recurring tic in subordinates, in which he rudely dispatches a free-spending lieutenant to encourage prudence in the others.

Go Russian, *phrase.* Temper tantrums as a negotiating tactic, derived from the experience of Western businesspeople whose negotiating partners sometimes "go Russian" and threaten to terminate discussions unless they get their way. "Negotiations [in Russia] are demanding and may become emotionally charged," said British negotiating consultant Sergey Frank. "You may find your Russian negotiator banging his or her fist on the table or leaving the room. Accept such tactics with patience and calmness. They are designed to put you off your stride."

gold talent, *n*. Capable but underutilized workers buried deep in the ranks.

golden coffin, *n*. Life insurance for the CEO who dies in harness, in which the deceased's outsized compensation lives on after him as payments made to surviving family members. If the departed was employed in a firm that extends lifetime employment even to mediocre workers, he had already been toiling in a "velvet coffin" for some time.

golden crumbs, *n*. Lucrative but tiny market niches ignored by the big players.

golden hello, *n*. Signing bonus of cash and stock options for young recruits in high-demand callings such as computer science and electrical engineering whose value exceeds the entire grubstake with which Henry Ford launched his enterprise.

golf, *n*. Primitive outdoor bonding ritual. The perfect ruination of a Sunday afternoon, according to Winston Churchill, but useful to executives as a character-assessment diversion to test the frustration threshold beyond which a partner is compelled to hurl metal rods into trees and rivers.

When people golf together they see one another humiliated. At least 95% of all golfers are terrible, which means that in 18 holes

everyone in the foursome will hit a tree, take three strokes in one bunker, or four-putt, with everyone else watching. Bonding is simply a matter of people jointly going through adversity, and a round of golf will furnish plenty of it.
– Geoffrey Colvin in *Fortune*, in 2001

gorilla game, *n*. A market susceptible to dominance by an 800-pound gorilla, as in beer (Anheuser-Busch), cola (Coca-Cola), razors (Gillette), computer operating systems (Microsoft) and perpetual publicity seeking with feckless ballooning stunts (Sir Richard Branson).

go-to person, *n*. Designated ball-carrier on difficult projects, ready and eager to do the impossible and with a track record of having done so.

granular, *adj*. Term for the gritty details, which bear scrutiny. Shareholder's query of the CEO: "I think we need more granularity about exactly why the comptroller has relocated to a country that doesn't have an extradition treaty with ours."

graphic jam, *n*. Internet bottlenecks that result in 45-minute delays while you download Rembrandt's *Night Watch* during a virtual tour of the Rijksmuseum.

grayhair, 1. *v.* A neophyte executive's gambit of advancing an idea behind a phalanx of seasoned colleagues. 2. *n.* At Internet start-ups, the token executive with a driver's license and previous experience in meeting a payroll.

greenlight, *v.* The turning point, when a manager gives her assent after succumbing to cajolery, gut instinct and a slide presentation.

greenwash, *n.* A company's participation in high-profile recycling campaigns to obscure its continued role in oil spills, clear cutting of forests and runoff to mercury-laden tailing ponds.

groundhog, *n.* Indecisive economist or stock market forecaster who pops back into her hole without offering a prediction.

grumpies, *n.* Acronym for grown-up mature professionals, a high-spending demographic group attractive to marketers, consisting of well-educated people age 29 to 45 who fret about health and diet, feel insecure in their jobs and pine for early retirement.

guardian angel, *n.* Your apologist in the executive suite. Should he lose his wings, you too will plummet to earth.

halo effect, *n.* A shimmering bauble among the trinkets, giving the whole lot a luminous aura. Cadillac once had this pleasing effect on Chevs and Pontiacs, until Caddies were eclipsed by BMW and Mercedes-Benz.

happy, *n.* A public relations professional. Those who work in product promotion are "chirpies," while those who toil in crisis management are "denialists."

hard skill, *n.* A quantifiable ability, like assembling a computer or changing a lightbulb, as opposed to a "soft skill," like knowing how to make people feel good about working harder and more creatively for no extra pay.

Has left to pursue outside interests, *phrase.* Has gone quietly, after signing a non-compete clause.

Has left to spend more time with his family, *phrase*. Has gone quietly, to the only place that will take him in.

headroom, *n.* 1. Growth potential. "We think there's enough headroom in the Internet as a channel that we can continue to grow pretty aggressively," said Greg Drew, CEO of 800.com, an Internet retailer, responding to reports in 2001 that the Web audience seemed to be peaking. 2. Expanded cranial capacity resulting from successful completion of challenging assignments. Sought by the employee whose stated desire is to enrich her intellectual storehouse but who actually seeks to brighten her prospects for advancement to more generous pay levels.

helicopter manager, *n.* Always overhead, blocking out the sun.

hemorrhage, *v.* Term for corporate losses that have passed the point of comprehension, obliging financial journalists to reach for the most alarming descriptive in the metaphor bank.

hindsight, *n.* The mourning after.

It's partly the structure of Wall Street, the nature of a boom economy, that you only understand deals when they go wrong.
  – U.S. investment banker Bruce Wasserstein of Wasserstein Perella & Co., in 2001

hold, *v.* Synonym for "sell" among stock market analysts, whose employers are reluctant to bad-mouth the shares of companies that are or might be lucrative underwriting clients. Of the 8,000 or so U.S. analysts' recommendations in 2000, just 29 were "sells." "If you see 'Hold' on anything that extends the time horizon [for the forecast price] out two or three years, it's a polite way of saying 'Slowest one through the exit door gets trampled,'" said Dan Deadlock and Christopher Gulka of the InvestorExpo website.

holloware, *n.* Highly touted software that is less robust than promised.

home office, *n.* Workplace where overhead, stationery supplies and keeping the dust bunnies under control is the employee's responsibility, and the only chance for adult conversation is with the deliveryman from FedEx.

horizontal loyalty, *n.* Fealty to one's calling or profession, wherever one practices it, rather than the pecking order, or vertical hierarchy, of one's employer. This is the animating spirit of soloists more concerned with the activities of fellow software writers, accountants or brand marketers elsewhere in the world than with the folks who toil outside their discipline elsewhere in the firm where they are employed. It presumes, by logical extension, that a cabal of, say, IT specialists or PR mavens, strategically placed at thousands of separate employers, could run the world better than a multifunctional team at one organization. The presumption failed its first test, the implosion of dot-coms – which were blessed with lots of programmers, and not so many marketers, bean counters or accounts receivable pros.

hot desking, *n.* A phenomenon of the unstructured, New Age office, in which productivity is supposedly enhanced by having employees toil wherever they want to in cubicleland, on the theory that if you abolish private space you abolish ego. In practice, you increase the incidence of people staying at home or heading out to the parking lot or local movie house for some solitude to complete assignments.

hourglass mode, *n.* Holding pattern while waiting for something to happen, inspired by the hourglass icon that Microsoft Windows uses to say it's too busy to take on a new task.

How may I exceed your expectations today?, *phrase.* Ask anything more difficult than the time of day and I'll have to get my supervisor.

hug merchant, *n.* An empathy peddler, notably the consultants on corporate restructurings who encourage ax-wielding CEOs to administer the blow with a touch of humility and compassion.

hyperflier, *n.* Very frequent business flier, who spends more time aloft than on the ground, and thinks nothing of traveling 6 hours across the Atlantic for a 30-minute meeting. The hyperflier has a pallid complexion, red watery eyes and a crease in the stomach from having a laptop crushed into her body by the reclining seat in front of her.

I

I bought a stock that doubled last year, *phrase*. The rest of my portfolio tanked.

idea hamster, *n*. Colleague who spins out new concepts without cease, leaving it to others to determine their feasibility while she builds a reputation for herself as an indispensable guru.

identity mark, *n*. A corporate logo generated from a computer-sorted list of 100,000 suggestions, tested on employees, clients, suppliers and shareholders, and unveiled in a multimillion-dollar marketing campaign. At which point a veterinary college in Nebraska must gently be persuaded to surrender its prior claim to an identical mark.

Idi Amin complex, *n*. Term coined by Columbia University professor Donald Hambrick, and inspired by the former

Uganda dictator, to describe the corporate autocrat who insists on holding all three top posts – chairperson, chief executive and president.

I did my research on this stock, *phrase*. I tried one of the company's products.

I don't need a broker's advice, *phrase*. I can't find one who takes calls from people with less than $5,000 to invest.

I have a high-risk tolerance with stocks, *phrase*. I'm selling on the next hiccup.

I have a wonderful broker, *phrase*. One of the eight stocks he had me buy worked out, so I don't feel like a complete boob in paying for his yacht.

I'm well diversified, *phrase*. Besides the house and the car, I own three stocks.

impostor syndrome, *n*. An acute sense of the flukes by which you gained the high station for which you are not qualified.

Everyone who's running something goes home at night and wrestles with the same fear: Am I going to be the one who blows this place up?
– Jack Welch, CEO at General Electric, who actually did blow up an experimental power plant early in his career at GE

impropriety, *n.* A trifling illegality or breach of the corporate code of conduct not meriting the attention of the criminal justice system, although executive dining room privileges will be withheld from the wrongdoers for some time.

inactivity fee, *n.* Penalty imposed by the bank for your neglect in letting it deploy at will the deposits you appear to have forgotten about.

in-box dread, *n.* A form of morning sickness in which the patient reluctantly confronts an accumulation of overnight e-mails and messages not attended to the previous day, or month.

incent, *v.* The dispensing of stock options, performance bonuses, travel allowances and other bribes as a means of energizing employees for whom drawing a mere paycheck is insufficient motivation.

There's no praise to beat the sort you can put in your pocket.
 – Molière

Men will not do an extraordinary day's work for an ordinary day's pay.
 – Frederick Winslow Taylor, early-twentieth-century guru of production efficiency

income stock, *n.* A stock that pays a dividend, which excuses the fact its price has languished for a decade. Safer than a growth stock, whose lack of dividends is not a cause for sorrow until the capital gains it promised are erased in a market reversal.

info lush, *n.* An executive who consumes vast quantities of data as a stalling tactic before making a decision.

infraction, *n.* A modest breach of legal etiquette, settled with a small fine and a discreet apology published in an out-of-town newspaper.

infrastructure, *n.* Tools of the trade. In construction, a fleet of bulldozers. In e-commerce, a network of software, servers and storage systems. In defense contracting, a passel of retired admirals on the payroll. In Hollywood, a bankable director and a photogenic star.

innovation, *n.* 1. A copycat version of the market-leading product that doesn't too obviously mimic it. 2. A ballyhooed improvement on the original, which, after years of painstaking R&D work, is now available in family size.

input session, *n.* A routine summit of top-level executives that has been thrown open to middle managers, ostensibly with the goal of seeking advice from the front lines. At troubled companies, this is often an exercise in prepping lesser bureaucrats to take on the responsibilities of vice presidents who are about to be fired.

intellectual capital, *n.* 1. Ideas for rent or hire. 2. The collective brains, patents, trademarks and copyrights of the enterprise, examples being the gray matter between Bill Gates's ears, the Colonel's secret recipe of 18 herbs and spices, and those oversized Ronald McDonald lawn jockeys that line the I–95 from Maine to Florida.

internal growth, We are focused on, *phrase.* Even if we hadn't crapped out overseas, we no longer have the money to expand abroad.

internalizing the externalities, *n.* The carriage maker, noticing the reduction of horse dung in the streets, stops denigrating horseless-carriage enthusiasts and makes the switch to automaking.

inter-operable, *adj.* Compatible with other machines but not necessarily with humans.

investing opportunity, This is a great long-term, *phrase.* Be patient. Be *very* patient.

One thousand dollars left to earn interest at 8 percent a year will grow to $43 quadrillion in 400 years. But the first 100 years are the hardest.
  – U.S. stock market analyst Sidney Homer of Salomon Bros.

investment banker, *n.* Middleman whose cut from passing funds from investors to corporations is the only money still in evidence a year after the transaction.

An investment banker with a sense of fair play is one who honks before running over his competitor's grandmother.
  – *Brill's Content*

iteration, *n.* One of several drafts. The last iteration is the clarification issued after the release of the final draft.

It's a great company, *phrase.* It's been a lousy stock.

J

Jacuzzi effect, *n.* The propensity of people whose homes have been destroyed by hurricanes not only to rebuild them, but to add expensive amenities, such as decks and indoor spas, thus increasing both the value of their home and the demand for construction workers.

job search, unplugged, *n.* Old-fashioned job hunting, by poring over classified ads and wearing out shoe leather, without use of Internet websites like Monster.com and HotJobs.com.

The reality is that fundamental skills such as networking and interviewing remain critical to the job search process. The Internet can be a valuable door-opener, but the in-person interview is still the ultimate deal maker.
  – Thomas Silveri, chief executive of workplace consulting firm Drake Beam Morin

job seeker, passive, *n.* Disillusioned employee who will defect at the first decent offer, and in the meantime is a clock-watching drag on the operation.

judgmental lapse, *n.* Synonym for white-collar crime, used by corporate executives after an embarrassing outbreak of high-level executive malfeasance has come to light.

jumper, *n.* Executive from a traditional company who is lured to an Internet firm, mesmerized by the once-in-a-lifetime chance to play a role in the transformative impact of the New Economy – and to cash in a small mountain of stock options a few months after the IPO.

junk loans, *n.* Bridge financing provided by brokers to firms not yet ready to test the credulity of investors in junk bonds.

just-in-time employment, *n.* Chronic reliance on part-time and short-term contract workers, who often lack experience but need not be compensated with the full range of employee benefits.

just-in-time learning, *n.* On the shop floor, training in how to make the new machine. In the executive suite, training in how to manage a newly acquired business that is foreign to the company's prior experience.

K

k-commerce, *n.* Knowledge commerce. Consists of web trading in Rube Goldberg patents, conspiracy theories and academic exotica that otherwise would not find a publisher.

kevork, *v.* (after Michigan euthanasia enthusiast Jack Kevorkian). To terminate an idea, project or relationship. "I kevorked his e-memo before it could get onto the next IT agenda."

kickback 1. *n.* Modest reimbursement for the border official's more focused effort to interpret a bill of lading. (Also "speed money.") 2. Immodest bribe to draw customers into the showroom. (Also "rebate.")

kimono, Open the, *phrase.* Reveal sensitive information about the company to a prospective merger or joint-venture partner. Likely originated with the spate of Japanese acquisitions of high-profile North American assets such as Rockefeller Center and Columbia Pictures in the 1980s. "Before we open the kimono let's make sure these guys aren't just window-shopping or snooping for 'competitive intelligence.'"

kitchen-sink accounting, *n.* The decision to write off all the disasters at once, in hopes that the dizzying array of losses from the latest crop of mishaps will dissuade analysts from troubling to examine any of the fiascoes in detail.

Agonizing over errors is a mistake. But acknowledging and analyzing them can be useful, though that practice is rare in corporate boardrooms. Triumphs are trumpeted, but dumb decisions either get no follow-up or are rationalized. The financial consequences of these boners are regularly dumped into massive restructuring charges or write-offs that are casually waved off as "nonrecurring." Managements just love these. Indeed, in recent years it has seemed that no earnings statement is complete without them. The origins of these charges, though, are never explored. When it comes to corporate blunders, CEOs invoke the concept of the Virgin Birth.
– Warren Buffett, CEO of Berkshire Hathaway Inc., in 2001

knockoff, *n.* A rival's superior version of the pioneering product you brought to market before troubling to make it practical, safe, reliable and affordable.

knock-on effect, *n.* A sympathetic reaction. For instance, the advent of the personal computer not only gave us "wheels for the mind," as Apple promised, but also brought about finger cramping and anchors for the butt, inspiring the markets for ergonomic keyboards and chairs.

knowledge worker, *n.* A paper-shuffler or keyboard jockey with the good sense to take shelter behind a desk rather than risk life and limb in a mine shaft. He lacks the smarts to draw an ingot of steel without melting his left arm or to assemble the 5,000 parts of an automobile in proper order.

Knowledge worker: A person who has traded union protection for carpal tunnel syndrome or repetitive strain injury.
  – Eileen C. Shapiro, *The Seven Deadly Sins of Business*

Kool-Aid, She's drunk the, *phrase.* A true believer who, with messianic fervor, embraces a new order of things, exhibiting a cultlike intolerance of any contrary point of view. Lately used as a management tool at New Age tech companies, where employees regard their workplace as an experiment in changing the world.

Any journalist who dealt with Apple during the great years knew there was some other weird thing that went along with the Apple pride. Apple not only believed in Apple, it also believed in the

party line, and it expected everyone – journalists as well as employees as well as customers – to toe to it. Everything was great – except if you said it might not be. You were either friend or enemy. At Apple, business was personal. You had better believe.
– Michael Wolff in *Forbes ASAP*

kubris, *n.* Acute egomania tending to self-destruction, inspired by film director Stanley Kubrick and applied to cyber-world auteurs who commit stupendous sums to projects by which they expect to revolutionize an industry. Example: the failed multibillion-dollar bid by Oracle Corp.'s Larry Ellison in the mid-1990s to reinvent personal computing with hardware that never emerged from the lab.

kudocast, *n.* Employee-awards show broadcast on the company's internal TV network. Hi Mom!

L

last-mover advantage, *n.* Bonanza reaped by the few survivors in a mania such as the tech boom, who hold back from overinvesting in the early phase and are later able to conduct a mop-up operation by acquiring fallen rivals and their prized technology at a bargain price.

laurel and heartache, *n.* The tendency of corporate fortunes to tailspin after the CEO has come in for heavy praise in a *Forbes* cover story.

leading edge, *adj.* Still in test phase. Might someday work, might someday fill a market need. Has already done wonders for the stock price.

leak, *n.* An unauthorized emission.

Every memorandum will leak. Every memorandum marked "confidential" will leak even faster.
 – Robert Reich, secretary of labor in the Clinton administration

learning curve, *n.* How you came to know more and more about something you understand less and less.

learning opportunity, *n.* You will fail at this, but we won't hold it against you.

legacy product, *n.* The foundation of the company's early success, like soap at Procter & Gamble and mainframe computers at IBM, to which such firms are held captive, blinding them to disruptive new products from upstart rivals.

Older products tend to be more profitable than new ones – R&D costs are lower, and the sales effort is not as great since customers simply order upgrades. There's always a temptation to want to keep selling such profitable products. But the danger is that you're caught trying to improve the old stuff long after your customers have decided to move on to the next-generation products.
 – John Roth, CEO of Nortel Networks

level playing field, All we're asking for is, *phrase.* All we're asking for is the same unfair advantage the other guys have.

leveraged, highly, *adj*. Woefully indebted. Think fourth mortgage.

lifeboat discussion, *n*. Role-playing game in which managers rank employees for promotion, pay increases and retention by asking them to choose which of their colleagues they would want with them if stranded in a lifeboat. It's fun!

lighting indicator, *n*. Leading indicator of retail activity. A preponderance of apartment buildings where lights are blazing on pre-Christmas evenings bodes ill for shopping center sales.

litigation, disappointment, *n*. Lawsuits brought against employers for failure to cough up expense reimbursements, health insurance coverage, stock options and other goodies that were used to induce them to join a firm that has run aground.

logo scrunching, *v*. A theory, as yet untested on linguists, that removing the space between the words in a company's name imparts a *frisson* of dynamic efficiency to a plain-Jane enterprise.

The two words, Planners and Banc, were fused into PlannersBanc in keeping with the new lean, mean fashion of jamming names together with a capital letter sticking up in the middle ...

NationsBank, SunTrust, MicroHelp, HomeBanc ... as if that way you were creating some hyperhard alloy for the 21st century.
  – Tom Wolfe, *A Man in Full*

looky-loo, *n*. A web window shopper who looks and runs. Less annoying than an electron, a visitor who bounces all over a site with no evident logic and keeps his wallet shut. Or a detail diver, who might buy something eventually, but must first click each button on the site to see how everything works.

low-hanging fruit, *n*. The easy tasks. These include profit-enhancing and cost-cutting moves that are obvious and can be accomplished without difficulty. At which point the firm is obliged to hire a CEO with longer arms.

luxe, loony, *n*. Possibly misplaced belief that a $327,000 timepiece assembled by a wizened Swiss craftsman, and boasting 1,118 sprockets, fly rods and other moving parts, is more rugged than its $50 counterpart consisting of a silicon chip glued to a strip of snakeskin.

The owner of a really expensive watch isn't just saying "I'm rich and you stink." He's saying, "I appreciate quality and material integrity. You and your Palm Pilot are the mere electron blips of an ephemeral age."
  – David Brooks in the *New York Times*, in 2001

M

mallingerer, *n*. Bane of shopping-mall operators. A visitor with spiked fluorescent hair, a multitude of pierced body parts and a spending limit dictated by her parents.

managing the blood supply, *n*. Monitoring high-performance employees to detect early signs of anemia, in order to purge workers who have run out of ideas, lack initiative and fear risk.

managing up, *n*. Polite term for brownnosing. Keeping the boss happy by solving her problems and making it look as if she did the heavy lifting. And keeping your own employees happy by being a buffer between them and your boss, so it's only your tirades they suffer.

market bottom, *n.* The point of maximum despair, when greed is poised to make up some ground on fear.

market-driven, *adj.* Responsive to the needs of customers, not the whims of the designer, manufacturer, distributor or CEO pursuing a pet project.

market, Gentle Ben, *n.* Mild bear market, such as the brief downturns of 1987, 1990 and 1998, followed by a sharp recovery in share prices, rewarding investors who buy on dips.

market, grinding bear, *n.* A false spring, as in the stock markets of 1929 and 1973–74, in which share prices appear to be recovering only to plunge again, punishing bargain-minded investors who tried to buy back in at the bottom.

market top, *n.* The point of maximum euphoria, when sanity reappears and prices are poised to fall.

market we are targeting has yet to be fully defined, The, *phrase.* We have a concept but no customers.

marriage, starter, *n.* The MBA's brief fling with her first employer. Largely meaningless, save for useful on-the-job training in vital matters such as housing allowances, deferred-income plans and stock-option vesting practices.

massage, *v.* To rework the numbers until the project becomes agreeably viable.

material adverse change, *n.* A setback so devastating we didn't even think about trying to hush it up.

maverick, *n.* A failed visionary. Freddie Laker's pioneering idea for a renegade discount airline did not achieve profitability. He was a maverick. Sir Richard Branson's knockoff of Laker's concept makes money. He is a visionary.

meal bridging, *n.* In snack foods, the profit opportunity between lunch and dinner. With North Americans deriving an estimated 30 percent of their daily calorie intake from snack foods, Richard Lenny, CEO of Hershey Foods Corp., was eager to expand his product lineup beyond chocolate. "With all the grazing and meal bridging that's going on, we're certainly going to be looking across the broader snacking market."

media slut, *n.* Purportedly informed commentator, usually a journalist, securities analyst or money manager, who is available at a moment's notice to pontificate on the import of breaking news. These tribunes are admired by colleagues back at the office for managing to convey the impression of being steeped in real-world knowledge, when in fact they spend most of their time en route to TV studios.

meeter, *n.* 1. Indecisive manager who convenes summits as a stalling tactic. 2. An always-show at meetings, paranoid that a decision affecting her life might be made in her absence.

You can observe a lot by watching.
  – Yogi Berra

meeter mouth, *n.* A compulsive talker in gatherings, determined to have input on every agenda item.

The meeting ghouls: folks who, under the motto "I am busy, therefore I am productive," manage to maximize meeting attendance and minimize everything else – especially tasks that might involve real work.
  – Eileen C. Shapiro, *Fad Surfing in the Boardroom*

meeting, pre-, *n.* A huddle where participants identify likely antagonists at tomorrow's formal gathering, synchronize their stories to avoid contradictions among themselves, and assign wake-up-call duties.

meeting, recycled, *n*. A meeting to review what was discussed at the last meeting.

When I was a graduate student at Harvard I learned about showers and central heating. Ten years later I learned about breakfast meetings. These are America's three great contributions to civilization.
– Mervyn A. King, economics professor at the London School of Economics

meeting, town hall, *n*. Officially, a feel-good dialog with staff. Unofficially, the means by which executives satisfy their penchant for prevarication while issuing subtle threats to the unwillingly assembled.

memory pig, *n*. 1. A software program that looms too large on the hard drive. 2. A Cassandra who appears to have encyclopedic knowledge of every failure in the company's history, which he cites in shooting down ambitious ideas.

mentor, *n*. A superior who sees advantage in pulling you up the ladder behind her, not unreasonably confident that you will speak well of her leadership abilities to those below you.

I have lived some thirty years on this planet, and I have yet to hear the first syllable of valuable or even earnest advice from my seniors.
– Henry David Thoreau

mercenary manager, *n.* A peripatetic specialist in finance or marketing, often retired from a career in big business, hired to impart gravitas to a fledgling small business.

merger, *n.* An exercise in solving your own problems by purchasing someone else's.

Most megamergers seem to be based on an assumption that if you create a really, really big dinosaur, it will somehow survive extinction.
 – U.S. management-text author Gary Hamel

merger of equals, *n.* Label that a sensitive acquirer gives to the purchase of a company whose delicate culture it chooses not to disturb. Only later will it exile decision-makers hailing from the acquired firm, according to a plan devised well before the combination was conceived.

meritocracy, *n.* An organization where everyone has an equal opportunity to advance, regardless of race, gender, age, disability or sexual orientation, so long as they hit arbitrary sales, profit, market-share and other targets while sacrificing home life in blind obedience to their superiors.

metrics, nonfinancial, *n.* New Age methods of valuing stocks, which substitute ephemera such as website traffic, page views and "aggregated eyeballs" for customers, cash flow and cost control.

mickey, *n.* Unit of measurement, usually 1/200th of an inch, for tracking the movement of a computer mouse. Not to be confused with Mickey Mouse, the Mac user's term for Windows 2000.

microcap, *n.* Stock in a smallish company admired for its growth potential until adversity renders it a mini-microcap, or microcrap.

mission change, *n.* Moses switches to Plan B.

mission, critical, *adj.* Essential to the proper functioning of the product or completion of the task. For instance, the boss's signature on a requisition order.

mission statement, *n.* A honeyed call to arms – innocuous, inoffensive and interchangeable with those of other companies, hospitals, museums and so on. Longer versions set to music are effective as bedtime lullabies.

No group of people is more disciplined in the submission of their personal expression to organization goals than corporate executives.
– John Kenneth Galbraith

A bunch of guys take off their ties and coats, go into a motel room for three days, and put a bunch of friggin' words on a piece of paper – and then go back to business as usual.
– John Rock, general manager of GM's Oldsmobile division, on the origin of corporate mission statements

mistakes, You've been good at learning from your, *phrase.* You'll be able to put that experience to good use with your next employer.

momentum investing, *n.* The practice of buying stocks that are rising in value because they are rising in value, without regard to their underlying value – the modest nature of which is revealed in a sudden economic downturn.

monetize, *v.* To convert something into money – for instance, by turning a tree into a share certificate.

mood ring vision, *n.* A strategy that seems to change depending on where, when and with whom the CEO is discussing it.

Moonies, *n.* True believers in the latest management theory to catch the CEO's fancy. "I told them it was time to refocus on basics like cost control and meeting our ship dates, but the Moonies kept getting in the way with their talk about 'cross-disciplinary enabling.'"

mooning the giant, *n.* Feckless disparagement of industry titans by would-be Goliath slayers, as when Corel Corp. founder Michael Cowpland vowed he would crush Microsoft Corp. in the market for word processing software. Cowpland, who dismissed his Redmond, Washington, adversary as a slow-witted bully, waged a ruinous price war that was soon won by Microsoft.

moral hazard, *n.* Theory that people gain a false sense of security behind the wheel of a vehicle loaded with government-mandated safety features, and drive more carelessly as a result. And that banks and other important businesses deemed "too big to fail," and protected by a safety net of government bailouts should disaster strike, will be run recklessly as a result.

mouse arrest, *n.* Purgatory for violating an online service's rules of conduct.

muffin memo, *n.* At the outset of hard times, a directive from the executive suite to dispense with free muffins at meetings. A warning that the CEO has shifted to cutback mode but hasn't yet figured out what or who is dispensable.

multitasking, *n.* Originally a computer term for machines that can run several programs at once. Now more commonly referring to the high-wire act that finds the time-impoverished executive mom applying makeup, eating breakfast and conducting a conference call by cell phone while driving the kids to school.

My broker sold me this lousy stock, *phrase.* I begged to get in on the IPO.

My stock portfolio is pretty mixed, *phrase.* I don't really know what I'm doing.

N

name currency, *n.* The trading value of corporate monikers, as evident in the inflated share prices of companies that have changed their names to include the words "solutions," "systems" and "networks."

nebbies, *n.* People whose outstanding mortgages exceed the value of their homes as a result of plummeting real estate prices, turning once enthusiastic home owners into "negative equity baby boomers."

negative cash flow experience, *n.* More cash going out than coming in. The income statement will soon reflect more proceeds from abrupt asset sales to gain liquidity than from profit generated by ongoing operations.

negative externality, *n*. Collateral damage, as in secondhand smoke from tobacco users, airplane cabin noise from travelers with children and time lost in convenience store lineups waiting for gamblers to select winning lottery tickets.

negative-growth quarter, Think of it as a personal, *phrase*. You're fired.

negative net worth, *n*. Insolvent. Just waiting for a bankruptcy judge to make it official.

negatively overshoot, *v*. In a broad market decline, the tendency of stocks to plummet below their inherent value as investors stampede for the exits.

The deluge of profit warnings issued by tech firms combined with a generally dimmed view of the economy has caused stock prices of several companies to negatively overshoot.
— Victor Halpert, analyst at Salomon Smith Barney, in 2001

nerd birds, *n*. Direct flights from San Jose in Silicon Valley to other tech capitals, including Boston, Austin and New York. The dress code is jeans and bomber jackets, even in first class. Soon after takeoff, the eerie glow of 60 laptops and a mood of paranoia fills the cabin, a fertile ground for espionage that accounts for the hushed voices and furtive glances.

netiquette, *n.* Informal standard of good manners on the Internet, where users are expected not to shout in ALL CAPS, dispatch overlong tracts that take forever to download or pass along offensive jokes unless they're *really* funny.

New New economy, *n.* An unforgiving era in which tech start-ups are required to find a way to make money – a prosaic successor to the New Economy, in which it was sufficient for a new technology to hold the promise of changing the world.

newsgroupie, *n.* An habitué of web chat rooms, or newsgroups.

next-business-day, on-site service, *n.* A peace-of-mind feature offered with your computer purchase for a modest additional charge. How it works: You log on to the vendor's website and have your problem misdiagnosed by its software. You go on hold for several hours waiting to speak to a tech rep, who will need much convincing that you really must have a new part, and will surprise you by explaining that software, keyboards, monitor and mice are not covered in the service contract. The technician finally appears on your doorstep, with the wrong part and another surprise: If your hard drive is replaced, it's up to you to restore your lost data.

next generation, *adj.* An imminent, bug-free and cheaper version of the product you just bought at an inflated price.

NHL opportunity, *n.* No heavy lifting required. Applies, for instance, to the fund manager who instead of researching the companies she invests in, simply bets on widely rumored takeover targets, ensuring a comfortable return.

nice-to-have's, *n.* Luxuries thought to be dispensable in hard times, such as the department you work in, where a fire sale of cubicles and mini-fridges could arrest the current share-price decline by at least half a point.

We're not spending on the nice-to-have's, capitalwise. We've delayed a whole bunch of office buildings and parking garages and things that are not essential.
– Craig R. Barrett, CEO of semiconductor giant Intel Corp., in 2001

non-compete clause, *n.* Severance package stipulation that the departing executive will either seek employment in an unrelated field or stay home and collect "hammock pay."

Norse, *v.* To conceive a brand name meant to invoke Nordic purity, as in Häagen-Dazs and Frusen Gladje ice cream.

Volvos provide a solution to a dilemma facing many academics – how to enjoy the benefits of increasing affluence while simultaneously maintaining the proper attitude of disdain toward the goods

that affluence brings. In the context of this dilemma, the ugliness of the Volvo becomes its most attractive feature, for it allows those who own one to plead innocent to the charge of really wanting a nice car. We don't buy these big expensive luxurious cars because we want to be ostentatious; we buy them because we have to if we want to be safe.
— Duke University's Stanley Fish, on the love affair between professors and Volvos

noun, collective, *n.* All-embracing term for a group of professionals. To wit, these suggestions from James Lipton in *An Exaltation of Business and Finance* (1995): A column of accountants, a riddle of economists, a meddle of micromanagers, an oversight of directors.

Nuremburg-style meeting, *n.* Rousing pep talk with exhortations to crush the competition, complete with props giving evidence of early success – including three guys hugging the rear wall who just defected from the enemy camp.

What do you do when your competitor is drowning? Get a live hose, and stick it in his mouth.
— Doug Ivester, president, Coca-Cola Co., in 1996

off-cycle salary adjustment, *n.* An *ad hoc* raise. These random pay hikes, outside the annual salary review, are among the first frills to be abandoned in times of austerity.

offline, *adj.* 1. Unconventional, off the beaten track. "None of our conventional approaches is working. The only way we're going to come up with a stroke of genius is to start thinking offline." 2. Private, in confidence. "Let's take this offline" (talk about it in private). "Why don't you folks settle that one offline?" (and stop disrupting our meeting with it).

offline retailer, *n.* Bricks-and-mortar merchant, where the shopping experience is not interrupted by computer crashes.

off-message, *adj.* A departure from the current orthodoxy as articulated by the CEO, adherence to which is required of her lieutenants. "Maybe it was just a slip, but no sooner do we convince Wall Street we're focused on domestic markets than Bill goes off-message with his blather on CNBC about reviving our global expansion."

offsite, *n.* A meeting at the nearby Ramada. A humdrum, one-day affair. Not to be confused with a retreat, where golf, a booze-up and a sleepover may be involved.

off-the-books compensation, *n.* Random treats dispensed by benevolent managers, including time off for good behavior, an expense account–funded luncheon for the project team and a two-week training session in Aruba.

on the beach, *adj.* Between assignments, jobs or careers. By cruel circumstance, a person so afflicted is not on the beach at all, but is at home sulking in his La-Z-Boy waiting for the phone to ring with an offer that tears him away from "One Life to Live."

110 percent, *n.* Minimum effort said to be required of the dedicated employee in the twenty-first-century economy. More proof that basic math skills are not the forte of consultants in employee motivation.

open-door policy, *n.* Archaic practice in which the CEO forced himself to listen to employee gripes in person. The modern

CEO need only make his e-mail address available to all employees to appear accessible.

I made a last attempt to be helpful, suggesting that the CEO use her full name, "Patti Hart," in her e-mail address, because the form she was using had an unfortunate pronunciation. The reply said that my note would not be passed on because Ms. Hart was accepting "revenue generating messages only." Until she left to become CEO of Excite@Home, she still used her old "phart" e-mail.
  – Jeff Raskin, computer system design consultant and father of the original Macintosh project, which he named after his favorite apple

opportunity horizon, *n.* Ambit of mischief, the full range of mistakes to which the firm has not yet committed itself.

optionaire, *n.* A millionaire on paper, who prays that the blush of investor enthusiasm that accompanied the initial public offering will last until her options vest.

options junkie, *n.* High-maintenance executive who must be "incented" with a new pile of stock options for each additional responsibility, such as making it to the office on time, replying to e-mails, deciding what to wear for the annual meeting.

organic growth, *n.* Attention to existing operations, having botched the acquisitions.

orphan, *n.* A neglected product lacking parental support, whose health flags as R&D and marketing funds are withdrawn.

out front, *adj.* Leading the vanguard in advancing a new idea. Way out front: There is no vanguard, just you.

outplacement consultant, *n.* A grief counselor who prepares executives for termination and walks them over to the other side.

outsider CEO, *n.* A leader recruited from afar, free of the organization's bad habits and carrying no baggage – save what he lugs in from former haunts.

We used to be so inbred it's a wonder we didn't have an eye in the middle of our foreheads.
 – Bill Salter, executive vice president at Sears, Roebuck & Co., on bringing top talent into the firm from outside

overbooked, *adj.* Celebrity CEOs such as Jack Welch and Donald Trump who attract biographers the way picnics pull in ants, a trend that began with Chrysler savior Lee Iacocca's monster bestselling memoir in the 1980s. Investor Warren Buffett is the subject of 16 titles, none of them written by the man himself, including Robert B. Miles's *101 Reasons to Own the World's Greatest Investment* (Wiley, 2001), which breathlessly describes Buffett's Berkshire Hathaway Inc. as "the umbrella during the rain, the skis and sled to navigate through the snow, and solid storm shelter during any tornado, hurricane, or typhoon." (Buffett describes the firm as simply a holding company based in Omaha.)

overbought, *adj.* Panic buyers have sent this stock to the moon.

oversold, *adj.* Panic sellers have pummeled this stock to dust.

own, *v.* To take responsibility for a project and ultimately the blame or credit, depending on the outcome and the political skills of the owner. "He owned it until the focus group results came in, then he'd never heard of it."

P

panic, *n.* Dated term for a massive reversal in the stock market triggered by a sudden widespread loss of investor confidence. The modern term is honking big correction.

panic, buying, *n.* A stampede to buy stocks before the price goes up, causing the price to go up.

Insanity in individuals is rare – but in groups, parties, nations and epochs, it is the rule.
  – Friedrich Nietzsche

It's like a balloon looking for a pin.
  – A U.S. fund manager in 2000, wary of a looming end to the tech-stock bubble

pantyhose jobs, *n.* Vocations in public relations, human resources and other realms of the pink-collar ghetto, where authority and promotions are limited but not so opportunities for taking the blame.

paper profit, *n.* Bonanza harvested by commercial printing firms during periods of record activity in the distribution of prospectuses for initial public offerings.

parachute, golden, *n.* Lucrative exit package to soften the landing for a CEO who is axed after his company, upon combining with another firm, finds itself with a spare CEO. Distinct from "severance protection," a sort of failure insurance negotiated by the incoming CEO to protect himself from a board with the courage to dismiss an incompetent helmsman. Go-away packages for the sacked CEO include at least two times his annual salary, accelerated vesting of stock options and a face-saving consulting contract.

paradigm, *n.* The way things used to be done, are done now, or could be done. A vaguely scientific term poorly understood even by the physicists who originated it, and a crutch for babblers whose ideas would provoke ridicule if expressed in plain language.

"I'm afraid that's a sunk cost, Charlie ... At this point the whole paradigm has shifted." Charlie started to remonstrate. Most of the Wiz's lingo he could put up with, even a "sunk cost." But this word paradigm absolutely drove him up the wall, so much so that he had complained to the Wiz about it. The damned word meant nothing at all, near as he could make out, and yet it was always "shifting," whatever it was. In fact, that was the only thing the "paradigm" ever seemed to do. It only shifted.
– Tom Wolfe, *A Man in Full*

parking lot, *n.* A place to route distracting ideas that come up in meetings, on a flip chart or white board, to be revisited later when exhausted participants are eager to dismiss them.

passenger, *n.* Someone who's just along for the ride, taking no part in helping drive the business yet quick to offer sharp critiques of those who do.

pay for performance, *n.* 1. Scheme for tying worker compensation to corporate performance by paying employees largely with stock rather than cash. In hyping the stock, the CEO seeks the twofer of inflating his own stock holdings and keeping a lid on wage demands by boosting the value of stock that has been given to the rank and file in lieu of folding money. 2. Scheme for rewarding the CEO with a swollen bonus and dirt-cheap stock options when times are good, and with a smaller bonus and even cheaper options to ease her pain when times are not so good.

peel or rip, *phrase.* Dilemma facing the CEO who has to decide whether to gradually shed poorly performing assets or dump them all at once, with attendant howls of pain from abandoned employees.

PDA, *n.* A clunky, unhandsome device meant to convey the impression that your work life is organized. The personal digital assistant is only a slight improvement over the traditional personal assistant, who didn't travel well, if at all, and was brutally candid about your wardrobe.

People are our most valuable resource, *phrase.* There, I said it. Now get back to work.

It turns out I was wrong. Money is our most valuable asset. Employees are ninth.
 – Scott Adams, *The Dilbert Principle*

percenter, *n.* Talent agent for CEOs, who negotiates the groaning compensation-and-perks package with the hiring firm's headhunter.

percussive maintenance, *n.* A whack upside the hard drive or any other machine that misbehaves, as set out in the instruction manual. (Fig. 7: Using the ax, carefully cleave the keyboard in two, and scatter the pieces about the room.)

philanthropy, strategic, *n.* Corporate donations funded from the advertising and promotion budgets. There are strings attached, including free performances by a grateful orchestra for staff and clients, prominent mention of the donor in posters at the music hall and in newspaper ads, and renaming of the event to incorporate the donor's name.

In the U.S., doing good has come to be, like patriotism, a favorite device of persons with something to sell.
  – H. L. Mencken

Charities are noticing that their corporate donors are more aggressive about splattering their names on anything the cause has in public view, and vice versa, putting the charity's name on corporate ads as a sort of endorsement. It makes no difference that toiletries have nothing to do with endangered species. Everybody likes animals and maybe the toiletry company can use that to help people like their products. So a toiletry company might pay to put the World Wildlife Fund in its ads.
  – *Barron's*

pink slip party, *n.* In California's Silicon Valley and New York's Silicon Alley, a boisterous networking fete that takes place about 8 months after the party to celebrate the initial stock offering, and attended both by laid-off tech workers and engineering-starved employers. In the Rust Belt, a post-downsizing beer-and-egg-swallowing contest at a local roadhouse, followed by a spirited discussion about who is to slash the tires of management cretins.

pipeline, *n.* 1. Network of copper and fiber-optic lines that connects Martha Stewart's kitchen in Westport, Connecticut, with your cold-water flat in South Central L.A. 2. Device for transporting dinosaur remains in Alaska for use in heating the homes of New Englanders, and for stimulating the philanthropic urges of donors to the Sierra Club and World Wildlife Foundation.

pitch coach, *n.* Also known as presentation trainer. Someone to prep you for your big pitch to the board. You will be warned about hostile body language, failure to make eye contact and the need to make sure you "Tell them what you're going to bore them with, bore them, then tell them what you bored them with." Not to be confused with pitch gofer, the assistant vice president who schlepps your charts, graphs and handouts after pulling an all-nighter proofreading your PowerPoint presentation.

planning cycle, *n.* Seek approval for budget. Make do with smaller budget than sought. Try to justify going over budget. Advise successor to seek four times, not twice, what she needs in budget. Early-retirement gift: calculator in lieu of gold watch.

plastic surgery, *n.* Process by which spouses and financial institutions relieve debt-burdened consumers of their overused credit cards, in the interest of fiscal fitness.

platform, *n.* A business model dressed up by consultants. Every new project, branch office and acquisition is a new "platform" for grinding out additional profits – or a diving board, in the case of particularly risky ventures.

play to win, *v.* And if that doesn't work, play just to get by. It works for General Motors.

When Karl Wallenda, patriarch of the Flying Wallendas, was in his seventies, he fell 120 feet to his death while trying to walk a tightwire between two office buildings in Puerto Rico. Later, his wife said that before the stunt, for the first time in his life, Karl had seemed concerned about falling. When it came time to perform, he fell because he was so focused on not falling, rather than on getting to the other side. In tough times, remember Karl Wallenda.

When you concentrate on not losing, rather than on winning, you'll find yourself dead on the ground.
– Warren Bennis, business professor at the University of Southern California

Please hold, we are experiencing higher-than-usual call volumes, *phrase.* You might wonder, why aren't we experiencing higher-than-usual staffing volumes?

plug and play, *adj.* An acquisition whose balance sheet, technology and personnel require no adjustments to fit in with the acquiring company. "The idea is that when we bring in these companies, they can plug and play," said Alain Belda, CEO of Alcoa Inc., describing the aluminum company's search for acquisitions where no post-takeover re-assembly was required. The term also applies to new hires. "Cindy was up to speed from the moment she got here, no training required. A real plug-and-player."

port, *v.* Move, transfer to, translate into. "Stock options don't port to unionized workers – they want to be 'incented' with cash up front."

post-operative, *adj.* The point of maximum efficiency at the firm where a turnaround has just been successfully completed, before the accumulation of deadwood begins anew.

power aisle, *n.* The main drag of the store, where the overpriced impulse buys are stocked. Beyond it are "power walls," gaudy displays to draw shoppers to the emporium's deepest recesses.

power lounging, *n.* Prolonged downtime, sometimes lasting several months and including sabbaticals and exotic holidays, that hard-driving executives and professionals take to avoid burnout. Replaces the two-day absences that passed for vacations among type A personalities in earlier times.

powered, *v.* The forced disposal of assets through power of sale, especially property. "Apart from the country club membership, everything was powered. We lost the houses, the condo partnerships, the film units, the boat …"

prairie dogging, *n.* Response to commotion at the cube farm, as heads pop up over cubicle walls to see what all the yelling's about.

praiser, *n.* Author of the brokerage report that convinced you to buy the overhyped stock. Originally a term for publicists at Hollywood studios, whose integrity does not suffer by comparison with the Wall Street analysts who pump out flattering nonsense about companies for which their employers have underwritten stock.

preannouncement, *n.* Corporate disclosure of preliminary financial results a few weeks before the news is made official, in order to give securities analysts who have been touting the stock some time to take cover.

pre-families, *n.* Disney-talk for single people, a less lucrative source of theme-park revenue than visitors with ankle-biters in tow.

pre-IPO, *adj.* State of grace in which an enterprise's dim prospects for turning a consistent profit are still a closely guarded secret among the firm's founders. "Today almost all of the risk has been moved to the public markets," reported Silicon Valley's *San Jose Mercury News* in 2000, "giving unprecedented returns to everyone in the pre-IPO daisy chain, from founders and option-holding employees to venture backers to the investment bankers who handle the offering."

pre-loved, *adj.* Cloying version of "pre-owned," a come-on in the classified ads for used luxury items.

premature accumulation, *n.* Bad timing on the part of the impetuous investor, who snaps up undervalued shares in a company with good, long-term prospects, just before those shares suffer a further, short-term fall in the market.

pre-revenue stage, *adj.* Nowhere to go but up. Still raising money for office supplies and first and last month's rent. Next phase: "pre-profits stage." At this rate, investors can be strung along for years not expecting to see a dividend.

price objective, *n.* Optimistic share-price target set by stock market forecasters.

Why set price targets for a given year? Analysts should issue a lifetime price target for stocks. Yahoo! may hit $300 some decade, although most of us may not be alive to see it.
   – James F. Mitchell of Los Angeles in a 2001 letter in *Barron's*

price point, *n.* The right price for attracting the target market. An upscale ice cream bar priced at $1.50 looks like an economy item putting on airs. But at $2.75, the item is attractively decadent. "Must be good – they want $2.75 for it." The science of inflated pricing in watches is the entire underpinning of the Swiss economy.

If you don't charge enough money that they are conscious of it, you have no impact.
   – Management guru Peter Drucker, on his consulting fees

priced for perfection, *adj.* Description for a stock that's reasonably priced if every single one of the countless hopeful expectations for it is realized.

proactive, *adj.* Referring to an action that anticipates future conditions. Originates with the most recent genuine breakthrough in strategic planning, when cavemen first elected to gather kindling before the need arose to build a fire.

profit maximization, *n.* Cost minimization. There are more creative ways of maximizing profits, but cutting costs is the crowd pleaser best suited to the manager in a hurry to become a hero.

profitability, operational, *n.* Not the real kind, but earnings before taxes, depreciation and interest payments on the company jet.

profits recession, *n.* Abrupt end of growth in corporate profits, but short of actual losses, triggering an erosion in stock prices. Despite the rescue effort of central bankers in cutting interest rates, "the odds are pretty good we'll have a profits recession," said Chuck Hill, director of research at First Call, which tracks analysts' forecasts. In a "profit panic," share prices plummet in anticipation that earnings will disappear altogether.

pro forma earnings, *n.* In a prospectus touting a new stock offering, the company's anticipated profits over the next few years if reality fails to intrude on the firm's glowing projections.

profundicator, *n.* Windy colleague who must turn the simplest concepts into numbing gibberish.

propeller-head, *n.* A computer programmer. Suspected of dropping in from outer space, she alone in the office has a good excuse for speaking in code.

prospectus, *n.* Advertising flyer for a stock offering. A catalog of anticipated blessings and cautionary "risk factors." It is commissioned by investment dealers and written by lawyers at the requirement of securities regulators and stock exchange officials, who collectively represent its sole audience, investors having opted for guidance from "Wall Street Week with Louis Rukeyser."

George Orwell once blamed the demise of the English language on politics. It's quite possible he never read a prospectus.
– Arthur Levitt Jr., chairman of the U.S. Securities and Exchange Commission, in 1996

protected employee, *n.* A worker shielded from indiscriminate firing by anti-discrimination laws because he or she is 40 or older, pregnant, has children, is married, female, gay, disabled, non-Caucasian, religious or was born in another country. Given the foregoing, the chief means of avoiding a lawsuit for wrongful dismissal are to (a) fire no one or (b) fire everyone, or at least everyone in the same division, since the more employees who are treated the same way the more difficult it becomes for them to claim discrimination.

public relations, *n.* A happy-talk pantyhose ghetto, often a launching pad for marriage to the CEO (i.e., AOL's Steve Case, Microsoft's Steve Ballmer, Brascan's Jack Cockwell, designer Calvin Klein). Which figures, since PR is one of the few direct reports to the big guy, and its job is to inform the outside world about his unalloyed virtues.

The pressure of public opinion is like the pressure of the atmosphere; you can't see it – but all the same it is sixteen pounds to the square inch.
 – James Russell Lowell, American essayist and diplomat

puked-out, *adj.* In Wall Street parlance, the point at which the stock market has finally bottomed out, every last investor having sold their every last share. In the most vicious of bear markets, where investors are punished every time they buy on short-lived signs of recovery, the sage buyer waits until no trace of optimism remains and investors are totally drained of their earlier euphoria.

pulsing the customer, *n.* Tactics for gauging customer opinion. Focus groups are one method. Noticing that your product has been marked down at Wal-Mart is another.

pure play, *adj.* Term for a company that strives to make money in just one field, in contrast to conglomerates, which are adept at losing money in several.

push technology, *n.* Software that enables stockbrokers, bankers, haberdashers and other people with something to sell to bombard e-mail users with "reminder" messages aimed at pushing them into placing an order.

quality control, *n.* Diligent attention to the elimination of blemishes and defects, insofar as it doesn't interfere with consumer demand for immediate gratification at a rock-bottom price.

query, *n.* A question that requires a crisp, finite response. Originates with the computer age, whose repartee is conducted largely by two-finger typists and victims of repetitive strain injury, for whom baroque, open-ended correspondence is not an option. A throwback to the telegraph era. "Attn: Jim. I don't know, I can't find out and I don't care. – Mike. CC: Everyone else."

quit date, *n.* Agreed-upon time for completion of the project, anticipating the point at which mass resignation to the hopelessness of the cause will set in, making further work on it a pointless cruelty.

quixotic, *adj.* Illogical quirks of a colleague that are decidedly at odds with your own peculiarities of behavior.

quorum, *n.* Decision-making body consisting of the CEO. The CEO is an able proxy for fellow directors whose nomination to the board he proposed, and for subordinates who look to his arrival each morning for confirmation that a new day has begun.

R

random, *adj.* Disorganized thinking; spotty analysis. "Karen has a focused, logical take on this. But Steve's all over the map. He's too random to drive this project."

rank and yank, *n.* Performance appraisal system that grades workers on vague criteria such as "career potential" (biased against older employees with a perceived difficulty in adjusting to new technology) and "mature judgment" (biased against newcomers), with the lowest-graded workers fired or reassigned to another job.

real time, *n.* Now. As opposed to faux time, the precious moments you squandered while pausing to contemplate what you're about to do.

realignment, *n.* Remedy for the problem of more employees than work.

reality check, *n.* Payment up front, by certified check.

First they say they lost the invoice. Then it's going to be reviewed by someone. Then it hasn't been coded yet. Then it's going through the billing process. Then it's on somebody's desk. Then it's to be paid. Then it's been paid, the check is cut, but the check is not signed.
– Ed Laflamme, founder of a landscaping firm in New Haven, Connecticut, on clients who "play the float"

reality distortion field, *n.* The obstacle course whose perils the gung-ho project team is naively ignoring in pursuit of an impossible deadline. "The tech's still primitive, the suppliers aren't in line and the market isn't primed. They're deluding themselves about the distortion field."

reassessing it, Don't worry, we're only, *phrase.* It's going to take awhile to kill this as quietly as possible.

reboot, *v.* Start over from scratch, all the work done to this point having lost any value.

recentralization, *n.* The decision to take back authority from soldiers in the field, who turned out to be no brighter than the dolts at head office.

recession, mild, *n.* Other people are laid off.

recession, severe, *n.* You lose your job.

recession, severe prolonged, *n.* Consultants on the dole.

recessionwear, *n.* White shirts, solid ties and muted colors, tending to brown and beige, replacing the print shirts, Goofy ties and fluorescent tones of happier times when casual office dress was encouraged. "Don't think of these colors as dreary," said menswear merchant Harry Rosen of the earth tones – variations on copper, mustard and olive – that characterize recession garb. "Think rich vegetable tones."

redemption, *n.* The investor's reward for her faith in a subordinated debenture.

re-engineering, *n.* The process of taking a company apart and putting it back together again with fewer moving parts – that is, employees.

We tend to meet any new situation by reorganization and attribute to this the illusion that progress is being made.
— Petronius Arbiter

refi, *v.* In consumer refinancing, cashing in on lower interest rates by taking out a bigger mortgage and using the cash for essentials like a second honeymoon in Fiji.

regret, *n.* Old English word for sorrow, weeping and lamentations, but not, alas, contrition. The sincerest form of non-apology permitted by the legal department. Make that "deep regret," if the matter has reached the press, and "profound regret" if it is before the courts.

relationship with two million customers, We have a, *phrase.* We have the billing addresses of two million people who bought something from us at least once, whom we're pestering to buy more stuff.

reliable, *adj.* Less prone to malfunction than competing products in controlled tests sponsored by the vendor.

rent-a-crowd, *n.* Also syntheticrowd, hired stand-ins who pose as customers at plant, store and restaurant openings. Not to be confused with the audience at shareholder meetings, who are not remunerated for their docility.

repetitive brain injury, *n.* Affliction of telephone operators, tech-support personnel, brokers with fretful investing clients and others numbed by having to answer the same inane questions over and over.

repositioning, *n.* The decision to offer a flagging product in a variety of colors, or to embellish it with imaginative features, or to market it as a bargain item at a lower price, or if all that fails, to stop making it altogether and go into the steel business.

reputational capital, *n.* Term used in the CSR movement (corporate social responsibility) for a company's accumulated goodwill arising from exemplary treatment of stakeholders. Useful in offsetting the fallout from chemical spills, product-liability debacles and other outbreaks of antisocial behavior.

resources, release of, *n.* Hasty disposal of extraneous plant, property, equipment and personnel.

respect, *n.* A common substitute for affection.

Strive for respect. If you want somebody to like you, get a dog. I've got two. I hedged.
– Albert "Chainsaw Al" Dunlap, who conducted mass firings at Scott Paper Co. in the 1990s

restructuring, *n.* The rushed dismantling of subsidiaries and divisions, often in the wake of a failed repositioning.

retreat, *n.* 1. Staged withdrawal from a strategic initiative gone awry, conducted by the architects of the fiasco. Retreat gives way to rout when the authors of the misadventure are finally canned so that their mischief can be more thoroughly undone by an imported turnaround artist. 2. Conclave in the tropics where a regimen of golf, fatty foods and intoxicating libations can be relied upon to sharpen the acuity of top corporate strategists.

retrophilia, *n.* A marketing ploy in which familiar icons of youth – Lego, Kraft Dinner, Broadway musicals based on the works of Dr. Seuss – are cannily repackaged as adult comforts.

revectoring, *n.* A sudden, sharp change in outlook, usually at a time of distress. "In light of the buyers' strike by customers, we have implemented a judicious downward revectoring of our revenue and earnings targets. We have also notified our creditors that they should revector their expectations accordingly."

revenue recognition issues, *n.* An epidemic of phantom sales, the condition suffered by a company whose anticipated revenue gains are undermined by a spate of cancelled orders.

reverse booker, *n.* Public relations type who pesters media outlets to get her CEO on television, where he can promote his business with the apparent objectivity of a guest recruited by the show's own booker.

reverse engineering, *n.* Having launched the enterprise, staffed it up, debt-loaded the balance sheet and wowed investors with a flashy IPO, the process of going back to determine if and how the firm's underlying premise can be turned into a profitable business.

revolutionary, *adj.* Capable of supporting a dozen books on the topic and a regular segment on CNBC.

Time was, businesses were content just to hype their products. Nobody felt the need to predict a global realignment each time they opened a Chevy dealership. Has anybody noticed that leaders of nations these days speak of bite-sized change, while 25-year-old dot-commers promise the Second Coming?
– Nicholas Varchaver in *Fortune*, in 2000

reward, psychic, *n.* Trophy, plaque, badge, certificate, praise memo, important-sounding title or other expression of gratitude that lacks monetary value. The term was conceived by someone who possibly failed to recognize that cash would also suit quite nicely as a boost to the psyche.

ring fence, *v.* Quarantine for a newly purchased operation so its problems don't infect the host corporation. Reporting on BP PLC's 1999 acquisition of U.S. oil firm Atlantic Richfield Co., Britain's *Sunday Telegraph* said, "The process of absorbing Arco will be ring fenced to minimize disruption to the group as a whole (all of the Arco directors will retire)."

"Risk Factors," See, *phrase*. A butt-covering enumeration in the new-stock prospectus of all the dire events that could render the investment worthless. "There is a paragraph in the prospectus of any new issue that will tell you that the company's edge is fragile," writes Adam Smith in *The Money Game* (1967). "A prospectus is a legal document written by a Wall Street lawyer, and its purpose is to cry so poor that no investor can claim at some time in the future that he was misled. The paragraph of this truism will say – translated from the legalese – something like this: 'The Company has obtained 244 patents on its Digital Datawhack equipment. However, the Company has Competitors which are far larger and have far greater financial resources than the Company. The Company's abilities to maintain its profits and to stay in business depend on the ability of its people to stay head of these Greedy Giants, to create new goods and services, and the Company isn't at all sure that it can do this in the future, but it will sure as hell try.'"

roach motel stock, *n*. Shares that are difficult to resist buying, and impossible to unload in a falling market.

road warrior, *n*. A foot soldier with no fixed address, whose heroic instincts are most noticeably aroused when harassing airline personnel for upgrades to first class.

rounding error, *n*. Who can be precise with all these billions?

runaway e-mail, *n.* Confidential message that the recipient inadvertently bounces to a friend, who conveys it to relatives, co-workers and complete strangers. "E-mails, alas, are circulated as easily as confetti in front of a fan," said Margo Howard, advice columnist for the online magazine *Slate*, "and anyone who isn't aware of this is a quart low."

S

saboteur, *n.* In the mind of the incoming CEO bent on radical change, any employee who hasn't gotten with his program. Those who have are scorned by loyalists to the old regime as collaborators.

salary, competitive starting, *n.* A fraction above minimum wage.

salary negotiable, *adj.* Lowest bidder wins.

scalded cat, *n.* An investor who bolts at the slightest sign of a market downturn.

scale, *n.* Size. Sheer brute force in the marketplace.

Scale matters, and bigger seems to mean better to most managers. Maybe it's critical mass, or technology and globalization, or

integration, or sheer vanity and ego, but there is a natural imperative toward scale.
– U.S. investment banker Bruce Wasserstein of Wasserstein Perella & Co., in 2001

screaming video, *n.* CEO pep talk broadcast on the in-house TV network.

screen curfew, *n.* Cutoff point for kids' use of TV, computers and video games prior to homework, bedtime or wholesome outdoor activities like hanging out at the mall.

screwdriver shop, *n.* A tech company without a tech heart – for instance, a computer-equipment maker that assembles boxes filled with components that are designed by others. R&D at such "virtual" firms is either farmed out or acquired through takeovers, and therefore "bolted on" and not well integrated.

If you contract out the crown jewels what are you left with after all? Outsourcing is one of those ideas that sound good on paper around the conference table in the entrepreneuring fantasyland of Stanford's business school. But the real world is all about actually selling something or delivering some tangible service to a customer and doing it better than anyone else can. It is hard to see how a crowd of freelancers can deliver what the real world demands.
– Jeffrey S. Young, *Cisco Unauthorized: Inside the High-Stakes Race to Own the Future* (2001)

scripter, *n.* The boss's speechwriter. Both the scripter and his texts are prematurely gray.

An interesting difference between the average pitcher and the average chairman is that the former knows he can't hit but the latter doesn't know he can't write.
– Daniel Seligman in *Forbes*, 1998

scut puppy, *n.* Team gofer who books meeting rooms, does the photocopying and hotfoots it to Staples for office supplies – an assignment that will appear on his résumé as "strategic administrative support." The job has its possibilities. When Intel Corp. was launched in 1968, one of future CEO Andrew Grove's lowly assignments from cofounders Robert Noyce and Gordon Moore was to lease office space for the new firm.

seagull manager, *n.* A flighty meddler who drops in just long enough to mess things up. The periodic interference of brothers John and Forrest Mars Jr. at candy giant Mars Inc. drove many talented executives into the arms of rival Hershey Foods Corp. Describing the Mars brothers, a former company executive told biographer Joel Glenn Brenner, author of *The Emperors of Chocolate* (1999), "They are the seagull management team. They swoop down, shit and fly away."

sector rotator, *n.* A money manager who chases rainbows, investing in chemical stocks when they are hot, then rotating into bank shares, then high tech and so on, never pausing long enough to reap maximum gains from any sector.

sectorwide spending crunch, *n.* It's not just us, our entire industry is on the skids.

secure, *adj.* No hacker would be interested in corrupting this.

security seepage, *n.* Risk posed to companies whose trade secrets are stored on employee computers that are preyed upon by laptop snatchers at airports. The integrity of such devices might also be compromised by their use in playing Minesweeper and Internet backgammon.

see-through building, *n.* A future high-rise condo, currently an untenanted office tower completed during a real estate meltdown.

self-toast, *v.* Commit a career faux pas, often in the form of a fatally contradictory argument or impolitic comment. "Then he brought up how we did this before but didn't try hard enough – like we all wanted to hear again about how we almost lost the company – and he self-toasted. No one was listening after that."

sell, *n*. Securities analyst's rating on a stock. Not to be used. The correct term is "accumulate," which means the stock is fit only for investors with the patience of Job; or "hold" (we've fallen out of love with this stock, so should you); or "neutral" (dump it when you get a chance); or "reduce" (get out now).

The big securities firms only downgrade a stock when it's really all over. They'll ride them to the bottom with "we loved it at $50, we really like it at $30, and it's a steal at $10." Then at $5, they tell you to sell.
– Kevin P. Tynan, securities analyst at Argus Research Co.

sell it or smell it, *phrase*. In grocery retailing, the need to move the merchandise promptly.

seller, motivated, *n*. A seller held upside down by his creditors.

serial decline, *n*. Sequential collapse, like a row of dominoes. For example, the bankruptcy of Pets.com meant hard times for dot-com suppliers like Oracle, who in turn stopped advertising on upbeat TV financial shows, which no longer quoted dot-com cheerleaders at securities firms, who were dismissed from their $500,000-a-year jobs on Wall Street. (Okay, that last part didn't happen. But some of them *were* cut from the bonus pool that year.)

share of stomach, *n.* The prize in the battle between Denny's and Pizza Hut.

shareholder rights plan, *n.* Management rights plan. A scheme by entrenched managers to keep their jobs by making the firm takeover-proof. The effect is to deny shareholders the chance to be bailed out by a predator seeking to oust the managers whose ineptitude made the firm vulnerable to a takeover in the first place.

shelf clutter, *n.* Proliferation on grocery shelves of supposedly new and improved products that are minor variations on the original, part of a "land grab" by the marketer to hog shelf space and crowd out rivals. This explains why there are 16 flavors of Eggo waffles, 19 varieties of Colgate toothpaste and 72 versions of Pantene hair-care treatment.

shiss, *n.* Irritating sound effect of the New Economy. In *The Dictionary of New Media*, author James Monaco defines shiss as "the increasingly common scratchy background noise that emanates from someone else's Walkman in an elevator, car or other enclosed space."

show-and-tell, *n.* A presentation in which you "tell" how the new software will reduce the need for IT support staff, and you "show" the severed head of an IT geek. Show-and-tell tips:

Know what makes this particular audience receptive. (Do I wear the moose suit?) Explain the benefits of what you're proposing. (Bring a photo-composition of the boss in medium-security stir.) Be clear about what you want the audience to do as a result of your presentation. (Pass a collection plate.) And use arguments that are both rational ("This is a proven method of profit maximization") and emotionally bonding ("Okay, ignore me – like I'm the only one who knows this miserable tub is sinking").

showstopper, *n.* The entertainer's *pièce de résistance*, but in tech R&D a potentially incurable bug that casts doubt over the scheduled launch date. "The other planets are aligned but the incompatibility with the Microsoft suite is a real showstopper."

shrinkage, *n.* Employees and customers with sticky fingers. Describing rampant theft at his Dominion Stores grocery chain in Canada, owner Conrad Black said the stealing approached "the profligate corruption of looters in a deserted city or even a deserted ship. It would be unfair to blame employees exclusively. They accounted for three-quarters of the theft, but customers took another $10 million. In one quarter, a Protestant minister, a Roman Catholic priest and a rabbi, each in a different province, were apprehended for shoplifting."

Silicon Wannabe, *n*. Budding tech center with designs on Silicon Valley's fabulosity. For example, Silicon Alley (New York City), Silicon Fen (Cambridge, England), Silicon Glen (Edinburgh to Glasgow), Silicon Bog (Ireland), Silicon Ditch (west of London), Silicon Valais (Switzerland) and Silicorn Valley (Fairfield, Iowa).

single-digit syndrome, *n*. Tendency for stocks that spiral downward into single digits never to recover, crushing the hopes of bottom-fishing investors. One U.S. survey of 1,900 publicly traded tech companies whose stocks fell to single digits between 1985 and 2000 found that only 3.4 percent rebounded to $15 or higher in the next year, and most of those that didn't recover in the first year never did.

skunkworks, *n*. Originally a clandestine division within a company, inspired by the covert "skonk works" distillery in Al Capp's Li'l Abner cartoon strip and first used by Lockheed as a code name for its secret airplane division in the Second World War. Now commonly used to describe a corporate R&D operation or an idea mill where corporate strategy is hashed out.

skyscraper curse, *n*. Barometer of economic pressure that sees a correlation between bids to erect the world's tallest structures and the onset of economic crises. Tall buildings are a leading indicator of overheated economies, as with New York's 50-story Metropolitan Life Building (erected during the Panic of 1907), Manhattan's Chrysler Building and Empire State Building (heralding the Great Depression); the World Trade Center near Wall Street and Chicago's Sears Tower (completed during an era of runaway inflation, and the worst economic downturn since the Depression); and the twin 447.3-meter Petronas Towers (coinciding with the 1997 meltdown of Asian economies).

sleep camel, *n.* Workaholic who power sleeps for two or three days, then draws on stored z's during a subsequent week of 20-hour workdays.

sleep mode, *n.* Default position in meetings, public-transit commuting and waiting for your computer to reboot.

sneakers-up, *adj.* The demise of so-called dot-com ventures, where investor hopes have failed to triumph over the lack of experience and fiscal probity among entrepreneurs barely out of their teens.

social network, *n.* Acquaintances within the firm who think, act and dress like you. They may not help you get ahead in the company, but at least provide some shoulders to cry on.

soft alliance, *n.* A joint venture, partnership or other loose arrangement where no one's in charge and confusion reigns. In a hard alliance – that is, a takeover – it's clear who's in charge and tyranny reigns.

soft landing, *n.* Originally the term for a gentle moon landing anticipated by astronautic journals of the late-1950s, first applied to economics in the 1973 recession. Also "downy landing." Describes widespread havoc in the economy, but so far not at your firm.

soft restructuring, *n.* The *ad hoc* process of discreetly dumping assets and raising cash, while publicly denying that a desperate corporate rescue mission is under way.

soft room, *n.* A casual-retreat space at the office. This could be a dingy cafetorium with a corkboard papered over with bulletins from moonlighting Tupperware salespeople and would-be cat donors, or a fully outfitted rumpus room with a big-screen TV, exercise machines, a pool table and pull-out beds. In either case, the point of such facilities is not leisure but the chance to get even more work done without the phone, e-mail and other distractions in your cubicle.

soft skill, *n.* A talent whose impact is difficult to quantify, such as listening, empathizing, team-building and mediating, as distinct from results-oriented skills like kicking butt (getting results from stubborn malingerers) and kicking ass (whipping the competition).

Sorry, my hands are tied, *phrase, n.* Come back when you've got an assigned parking space closer to the building.

space, *n.* The e-world's fancy word for industry or market. "We've got to start now if we hope to be the dominant player in this space." Not to be confused with outer space, where distant profits from e-commerce are said to lurk.

spellcheck, *n.* Computer application that compensates for one of the alleged failings of the public education system.

Just because e-mail tends to be more immediate and personable, it can't be casual. Sending e-mail riddled with misspellings is the same as wearing a shirt splattered with catsup. Sloppy e-mail gets tongues wagging about the writer's literal failings.
  – The Complete Idiot's Guide to Office Politics

Bosses tend to have the poorest spelling and worst grammar in e-mail messages, conveying the sense that they have better things to do with their time.
  – Bruce Headlam, Circuits section editor of the *New York Times*

spendorphin high, *n.* Protein blast similar to the endorphin rush from rigorous physical activity, and released during shopping sprees – cited by psychologists as the most common self-prescribed remedy for depression.

spin-prep, *n.* Coaching for the CEO prior to her encounter with the media. The goals are to fine-tune her patter, conduct a wardrobe check and remind her that unlike the sycophants on the payroll, an impertinent media interlocutor cannot be threatened with dismissal.

squatter's rights, *n.* Tendency of a gradually fading division that generates 50 percent of profits to command half the capital budget and brightest employees at the expense of other divisions with better growth prospects.

squint, *n.* A fiscal skeptic, often a bean counter. The prudent manager, confronted with a grandiose scheme, will run it past the squints before proceeding.

staminac, *n.* A sleep-starved overachiever.

There are days that I work 14 hours, but most days I don't work more than 12 hours. On weekends I rarely work more than 8 hours.
  – Bill Gates, founder of Microsoft Corp.

status signifier, *n.* A behavior that subtly betrays rank and privilege. High-status employees gravitate toward the head of the table and seldom speak during meetings. They take their time replying to e-mails, and send curt, one-line messages in order to minimize their contact with drones. Garrulous low-status employees, not so comfortable with their own authority, laugh nervously during meetings, for which they have made the coffee, and use e-mail to forward jokes, send greeting cards and use happy-face "emoticons" like (-: and :-).

stay-on bonus, *n.* An inducement for employees designated to be laid off to complete the vital projects on which they are working. The bonus should cover their living costs during the time it takes to sabotage their ungrateful employer.

stealth mode, *n.* Image of haplessness adopted by the start-up enterprise that soon will rip off its clever disguise as a debt-ridden firm with a muddled business plan, and startle the competition with its prowess. The gambit would succeed more often if entrepreneurs didn't work so hard on the first part.

sticky bottom, *n.* An entry-level job that workers can't seem to rise above.

stock, All of the bad news has been factored into the, *phrase.* Even the dumb money has fled.

strategic dialog, *n.* Shotgun wedding between struggling companies, spurred by their anxious creditors and preceded by hasty discussion about hoped-for synergies and who gets stuck with being CEO.

strategic empathy, *n.* Overt caring for customers and employees as a marketing tool. "When Sally got pregnant, she received a 15 percent discount coupon for our fine products – just one of the many ways we at Acme Pipefitters put into practice our belief that people are our greatest resource."

strategic repositioning, *n.* A careful, deliberative assessment of the business, and a decision it would do better with a different product, relocation to another city, a 90 percent reduction in staff and a new name, but that it should otherwise remain faithful to the caring values that gave it a distinct place in the market.

strategic retreat, *n.* Be No. 1 or No. 2, or get out.

Some people say I'm afraid to compete. I think one of the jobs of a businessperson is to get away from slugfests and into niches where you can prevail. The fundamental goal is to get rid of weakness, to find a sheltered womb where no one can hurt you.
  – Jack Welch on his success formula at General Electric

strategy, *n.* A plan, as opposed to the fumbling guesswork that informs most decisions.

However beautiful the strategy, you should occasionally look at the results.
  – Winston Churchill

Before you build a better mousetrap, it helps to know if there are any mice out there.
– Developer and media mogul Mortimer Zuckerman

stress puppy, *n.* A wound-up ladder climber.

It's almost gotten to the point where there's stress envy. If you're not stressed, you're not succeeding. Everyone wants to have a little bit of this stress to show they're an important person.
– Paul Edwards, chairman of British forecaster Henley Centre

The trouble with the rat race is that, even if you win, you're still a rat.
– Comedian Lily Tomlin

stretch goal, *n.* Stress goal. A demoralizing encounter with certain failure, presided over by a lunatic.

strike zone, *n.* In retailing, a high-traffic area where sales potential is greatest. The rack of Juicy Fruit at the checkout, for instance.

structural constraints, *n.* Harsh facts of life about which nothing can be done. For instance, taxes, regulations, bullying rivals, inflexible suppliers and the CEO's descent from a long line of marmots.

style purity, *n*. Money manager's folly in sticking with a preferred method of investing regardless of the market's changing fashions. "Style shift," by contrast, is the money manager's folly in *failing* to stick with a preferred investing method in which she has developed some expertise. By this conspiracy of diehards and dabblers, investors are spared the inconvenience of amassing capital gains that would have to be shared with the tax authorities.

The Dilly Bar is more certain to be around in 10 years than a single software application.
– Warren Buffett, owner of Dairy Queen, and a purist about avoiding tech stocks

The dark secret of investing, the one we like to forget, is that at bottom it is a way of going to the race-track without having to smell the horses. If a fund manager tells us he invests only in small-cap stocks, he should honor that statement. But by demanding he make the statement, by over-emphasizing stylistic purity, we are killing the fun factor.
– Maggie Topkis in London's *Financial Times*, in 1999

succession, *n*. Selection of the new despot. Formerly a genteel exercise conducted with discretion, now often follows a public beheading of the incumbent.

In this country we find it pays to shoot an admiral from time to time to encourage the others.
  – Voltaire, *Candide*

I like to buy a company any fool can manage because eventually one will.
  – Money manager Peter Lynch of Fidelity Investments' Magellan Fund, on his stock-picking strategy

sucker rally, *n.* A beguiling upturn in a falling market, whose brief recovery induces bargain-hunting investors to snap up distressed securities that soon drop in value.

sudden wealth syndrome, *n.* Hollow affluence brought on by ephemeral paper profits in one's stock portfolio, triggering a blaze of spending on luxury comforts. "They've bought the BMW, and they have the $3-million Simi Valley house. And they still wake up in the morning and say, 'I don't feel good about myself,'" said Stephen Goldbart, a San Francisco psychologist and cofounder of the Money, Meaning and Choices Institute.

supplier bingo, *n.* At companies in distress, the practice of paying only those suppliers that scream and shout.

support staff, *n.* Drones with no direct hand in generating in profits, which justifies their anonymity and modest compensation. This covers toilers in accounting, shipping, IT, human relations, public affairs – most of the payroll, in fact.

support team, *n.* Helpers in the successful project, who may or may not receive generous thanks from a team leader who has skipped up the promotion ladder.

swiped-out, *adj.* Credit or debit card whose magnetic strip has been worn away from excessive use. Sometimes confused with "maxed-out," for the holder of such cards whose exhaustion of cash and credit lines has triggered a fiscal meltdown that puts him in kinship with the treasurer of Argentina.

synergy, *n.* Theory that one plus one equals three in a merger, discounting the impact of conflicting cultures, duplicated effort, incompatible objectives and time wasted in learning the names of a lot of strangers who, like yourself, stand a good chance of being streamlined out of a job.

The best way to make a silk purse from a sow's ear is to start with a silk sow.
– Norman Augustine, CEO of defense contractor Martin Marietta Corp.

tailorism, *n.* The overturning of Frederick Winslow Taylor's time-and-motion studies, which regarded workers as mere cogs in an efficient, if monotonous, industrial machine. This has lately been replaced by a new "talentocracy" of free-agent workers who tailor their jobs to conform to their lifestyles, not the other way around. Denizens of the Free Agent Nation (estimated population: 33 million) are philosophical about being called on selectively and for only limited periods of time by efficiency seeking "large permanent organizations" (traditional employers).

takeaway, *n.* 1. Handout distributed by the presenter, tangible residue of an oral argument. (Also "leave-behind.") 2. The one powerful, crusading idea that the presenter wishes to leave with her audience, a concept so powerful that half the audience will awake that night crying it out to the moon. Or not. "My takeaway was that she believes it can be done, but we're not ready."

takeunder, *n.* The eager submission by a troubled company's owners to the first buyout offer that comes along.

target date, *n.* Earliest date for which completion can be promised without inviting ridicule. Not to be confused with the launch date, at which time a bug-ridden prototype is unveiled, or the drop-dead delivery date, when the first glitch-prone items are released to the world.

targeted ad buy, *n.* A marketing message aimed at likely customers, as opposed to profligate, unfocused shilling from every rooftop.

teardown, *n.* An executive mansion purchased with the intent of razing it in order to erect a still grander edifice in its place.

tech support, product, *n.* A toll-free phone number, an e-mail address, a stale website and a Helpful Hints brochure with text in seven languages, none of them plain English. "Your call is important to us, and is being answered in sequence. In the meantime, press 3 for Michael Dell reading from his book, *Direct from Dell.*"

telecommuters, *n.* The pajama-clad workforce, which communicates with the office by phone, fax and modem. This gives rise to a phenomenon known as the "empty desk syndrome" – a windfall realized by an employer in reduced need for office space, but accompanied by a nagging suspicion that it is subsidizing sloth among stay-at-homers.

telematics, *n.* The car as a data cocoon, outfitted with dashboard PC, satellite navigation and sensors that gauge the severity of impacts by adjusting air-bag deployment and speed-dialing an ambulance chaser.

testosterone poisoning, *n.* An exaggerated degree of maleness in engineering, securities trading, auto design and other fields. It is said to dissuade women from seeking work alongside colleagues whose after-hours diversions include building beer-bottle pyramids and blowing french fries out their noses.

The market is overvalued, *phrase.* I got scared and dumped everything before the rally.

The market is undervalued, *phrase.* I was too stubborn to cut my losses.

thesis vehicle, *n.* The untested automotive equivalent of a doctoral paper, which may or may not be accepted by the ultimate jury – consumers. Speaking of Chrysler Corp.'s newly unveiled Cirrus and Dodge Epic minivan, product-design vice president Tom Gale said, "They are primarily thesis vehicles for future products."

The stock will bounce back, *phrase*. Maybe it will be worth something by the time my grandkids inherit it.

Think outside the box, *phrase*. 1. Escape the four walls of your office to clear your head. 2. Cut loose, get radical, take a go-your-own-way approach to decision-making. Proceed at once, after getting the usual all-clear from Internal Audit, Legal Affairs, Human Resources, Health, Safety & Environment, the parking-lot attendant and the CEO's spouse.

In any large organization there are only differing degrees of restraint. And the fact that it is often self-restraint or self-censorship does not make it any less confining.
– John Kenneth Galbraith

An administration, like a machine, does not create. It carries on.
– Antoine de Saint-Exupery

A new corporate language has been invented to support people's need to believe that their work is actually an endless quest for novelty. "Outside the box," for instance, is to our age what "plastics" was to the 1960s. The one thing that is certain is that anyone who uses the phrase is as deeply inside the box as a person can be.
– Michael Lewis, author of *Liar's Poker* and *The Next Next Thing*, in 2000

360-degree feedback, *n.* Input the manager receives from superiors, subordinates and peers before taking a predetermined action she can now describe as consensual.

Thumb Nation, *n.* The population of gadget freaks who communicate by thumb, inputting messages on the miniature keyboards of wireless phones, pagers and e-mail devices.

thump value, *n.* Sheer heft of an annual report, 10-K filing or promotional press kit for prospective investors. Documents that land with a thud are a warning of current or future troubles. Fatter-than-usual financial documents are chock-full of writeoffs, special charges, wordy footnotes and self-serving explications. And investor kits bursting with glossy brochures, thick statistical reports and chirpy press releases are a hallmark of high-risk enterprises, which have a tougher selling job than the healthy firm that can skimp on reading material.

time famine, *n.* Technology glut that compels us to fill previously free hours checking e-mail, scanning the Web for useless information and crossing the Pacific for a half-hour sales call. Nothing a sustained brownout or airline strike couldn't solve.

Men talk of killing time, while it quietly kills them.
 – Dion Boucicault

time suck, *n.* A time-waster. Formerly "time sink." "I was locked up all morning in the time-suck chamber, enduring another of Larry's interminable slide shows."

time to market, *n.* Pace at which a concept goes through the stages of budget approval, product development, rigorous testing, design modification, focus-group feedback, market positioning, factory retooling, distribution-logistics modeling and near-complete obsolescence prior to its arrival in the showroom.

tin handshake, *n.* A puny severance package for executives whose misjudgments and profligacy have put the corporation in dire straits.

Tinker Toys, *n.* Impractical or silly assignments in management training sessions, the successful completion of which will have zilch impact on the company's fortunes or your own career prospects. Telephone equipment maker Lucent Technologies was still facing insolvency months after it hired a consultant to lead 2,000 employees in sessions where they crafted paper airlines, although the workers made some progress in unleashing their creative powers.

tins, *n.* A New Economy acronym for Type A couples – two incomes, no sex.

titlewave, *n.* Changing of the guard, a shakeup with innumerable promotions, demotions, reassignments and dismissals, and a consequent spike in the business-card budget.

ton of money, *n.* Literally, $908,000 in dollar bills, weighing a gram each. A ton of money is chump change in the merger game. With its price tag of $110 billion, the combination of America Online and Time Warner was a 135,000-ton transaction.

Never eat more than you can lift.
   – Miss Piggy

top-line management, *n.* An obsession with goosing sales revenue, with scant heed to mounting costs in staffing, R&D, advertising and distribution to support the extra business, so that little if any profit is made on each new sales dollar. The remedy, bottom-line management, aims not only to cut costs but abandon discount-addicted customers who aren't worth the bother.

touch skin, *n.* A face-to-face encounter to seal the deal, transcending cyberspace's lack of intimacy and thus commitment. "We've jawed over as many of the objections that we can by e-mail. It's time to fly their guys in here and touch skin."

tough but fair, *phrase.* Only sporadically belligerent.

He was unpleasant, untrustworthy, self-centred, self-obsessed, deceitful, conceited, greedy, authoritarian, reckless, irresponsible and morally dishonest, but not, to my knowledge, involved in anything criminal.

– Andy McSmith in a 1994 London *Observer* article, leaping to the defense of the late press baron Robert Maxwell, whom he once served as a press agent

tourist, *n.* Employee who signs up for off-site training in order to take a vacation from work. "We had maybe three serious students. The rest were just tourists."

train wreck, *n.* A multifaceted disaster, akin to the patient with multiple problems who ties up everyone in the ER. Usually caused by an odds-defying confluence of bad decisions and worse luck. For instance, the 2000 implosion of the dot-coms was soon compounded by massive indebtedness among profit-starved telecom carriers and suppliers, which spooked bankers and investors from giving money to anyone, tipping the entire economy into recession.

training, company-specific, *n.* The way we do things around here, as distinguished from what you learned in school and from your last job.

transformational, *adj.* Registering high on the corporate Richter scale, something that really shook up the place – or seemed to at the time, until it was superseded by the next Sermon on the Mount.

transforming insight, *n.* A hunch in black tie.

transient guest, *n.* A lone-wolf business traveler highly prized by upscale hotels. Not part of a gaggle of conventioneers, the transient is likely to pay the top room rate and forsake the crowded dining room in favor of the overpriced room-service menu.

transition year, *n.* The next 12 months are a writeoff – we'll be spending the whole time fixing everything that went wrong with the strategy we boasted about last year.

transparency, *n.* In developing world markets, a high-road approach to conducting business, free of corrupt practices such as bribery of customs officials and minor bureaucrats. In the developed world, a decision not to put politicians on the payroll until after they've left office.

transparent, *adj.* Financial performance, such as cash flow and profits, that is clearly visible, not distorted by obscurantist accounting methods.

I think the attraction of our brand is first of all that it is highly transparent. Investors can touch and see and feel the product. You don't have to be a technician to find out which advantage the products offer.
 – Fritz Humer, CEO of lingerie maker Wolford AG of Vienna

troll, *n.* An habitué of corporate and institutional websites who pens incendiary messages to provoke the host, such as the cyberguest who posts barbecue recipes at the newsgroup of People for the Ethical Treatment of Animals.

trust slug, *n.* Child of parents grown suddenly affluent through stock market windfalls, and lacking a strong work ethic. One cure, said Dr. Lawrence Balter, psychology professor at New York University and author of parenting books, is to expose them to poverty. "Even if your Range Rover drives you to the shelter, at least they can help dole out food and see people in need."

turnaround, *n.* A return to robust health after a brush with ignominy.

When you step into a turnaround situation, you can safely assume four things: morale is low, fear is high, the good people are halfway out the door, and the slackers are hiding.
 – Nina Disesa, chair of ad agency McCann-Erickson

24/7, *adj.* 1. Service that's always available, excepting periodic maintenance, system failure, traffic congestion, hacker attacks and staff shortages. 2. The leisurely pace of life at bureaucratic organizations, with their work regimes of 24 hours a week, 7 months a year.

twentysomething Internet entrepreneur, *n.* A paradigm-shifting genius and deserving billionaire in 1999; a distracted, undisciplined, hopelessly inexperienced yobbo who has to move back in with his parents in 2001.

U

unassigned, *adj.* Tag for employees laid off and invited to reapply for work, with little prospect of success.

undocumented feature, *n.* A flaw, bug or "design side effect." Like the fly in the soup, there is no extra charge for this unadvertised enhancement.

uninstalled, *adj.* No longer employed here. Originates with the voice mailbox, building-security badge, cell phone account, laptop password and other electronic entanglements from which a departing employee must be disconnected.

unproven business model, *n.* Prospectus-speak for "We're warning you, this thing could tank a month after it goes public."

upgrade, *n.* A make-up effort following the hyped software launch, with fewer defects than the alleged 65,000 bugs in the first release of Windows 2000.

up-sell, *v.* Get the customer to buy a larger size, a greater quantity or more features. "Can I supersize that for you, sir?"

usability champion, *n.* Employee who plays the role of a technology-challenged consumer, and whose protestations about inscrutable instructions and impractical features are entertained with impatient mirth and resoundingly ignored.

The language of some of those messages that come up – it just absolutely drives me crazy. They are flat-out incomprehensible.
– William Gates Sr., father of Microsoft founder Bill Gates, on what annoys him about personal computers

usage erosion, *n.* Decline in usage masked by no change in sales volume, but pointing to an imminent collapse in popularity, as with the subscriber to *USA Today* who no longer reads the paper but does use it as a sun visor for his computer.

V

value-added, *n.* The handy pamphlet that shows you how to plug it in, justifying the 30 percent increase in price.

value chain, *n.* Everyone who contributed to the final version, including the lab technician who first stumbled on it accidentally while researching the antihistamine properties of Mountain Dew, the product engineers who opted not to overdesign it, the squints who must have been in sleep mode when its budget sailed through their department, the marketing gurus who elected not to sabotage it with delays to test consumer reaction and the CEO who gave it the thumbs-up despite an infamous *Fortune* cover story that described his predecessor as a boob for approving a similar concept that flopped.

values-based management, *n.* Instead of running the company for the shareholders this year, let's do it for the empowerment consultants, on-site day-care agitators, eco-terrorists, workplace-safety whiners, subliminal-advertising conspiracy theorists and the church groups that want to run us out of Sudan.

vanilla application, *n.* A bland computer program that will do no harm but is, alas, of limited use since it has not been custom-tailored to the client's specifications.

vaporware, *n.* Originally a hyped product that never emerged from the lab, originating with a Windows release that Bill Gates announced in 1983 that was endlessly delayed. (A variation, "slideware," was software that existed only in the vendor's slide presentation.) Now refers to any fanciful notion that will soon be forgotten. "He's got the stats and some buy-in from the suppliers for this thing, but it's just vaporware to keep his budget from being cut."

venture capital, *n.* Investment funds that act as a nursery for promising start-up firms.

In the early days, pre-1995 or so, we [venture capitalists] were too small to destabilize the whole economy, but by 2000 we were wreaking havoc everywhere. Most large companies were losing their best and brightest managers as we sucked them away with hefty stock options and visions of multihundreds of millions of dollars. Everything we touched turned to gold. Hell, we took our mistakes

public! The investment bankers were our partners in crime; there were so many of them hanging around our offices each morning we had to disguise ourselves as FedEx delivery people just to get into our own offices. We raised bigger and bigger funds, and we told our entrepreneurs, "Go big or go home!" The fools – they believed us.
– Howard Anderson, founder of Yankee Group and YankeeTek Ventures, an early-stage venture capital firm in Cambridge, Massachusetts, in 2001

vesting in peace, *phrase.* An office drone's ability to endure sloth, incompetence, treachery and malfeasance so long as his stock options are above water.

videoconferencing, *n.* Once thought to be a threat to business travel, long-distance confabs conducted by TV, in which the participants have blurry images and gerbil voices.

There's no value in a fuzzy picture of people sitting around a conference table. I spent $50,000 installing a system, and now I don't even bother going into the conference room to use it. I'll give you the whole thing for the price of hauling it away.
– T. J. Rodgers, founder of Cypress Semiconductor

viral marketing, *n.* Synthetic gossip in the form of e-mails created by marketers whose message is so compelling that recipients will pass it on to all their friends. By e-mail word-of-mouth alone, distributors of the 1999 surprise hit film *Blair Witch Project* managed to build the false impression that the movie was a real-life documentary. The tactic soon got out of hand. "If viral marketers have their way, in addition to my daily dose of e-mails from companies pitching junk, I'll get another pile passed on by friends," complained *Business Week* technology columnist Ellen Neuborne. "It'll be cute once, maybe twice. But there's a viral traffic jam lurking just a few clicks down the information highway."

virtual integration, *n.* Rare harmony among company, customer and supplier, coined by Michael Dell to describe how Dell Computer outsources deep thinking about new-product development to its clients and shifts inventory costs to suppliers, freeing itself to focus on marketing copies of the founder's memoir.

visibility, *n.* The view from the crow's nest, which may be shrouded in fog. "I'd like to give you a projection of our third-quarter earnings, but we have no visibility about 3Q order uptake." Translation: Our customers have stopped taking our calls, so we don't know if they're in a mood to place or cancel orders. We basically can't see our hands in front of our faces.

visionaries, peripheral, *n.* The CEO's retinue of flacks, bag-carriers and yes-men.

visionary, *n.* A CEO whose mildly subversive nostrums entertain the press, and whose tactics have failed to destroy the company through three business cycles.

visual aid, *n.* A prop for making a presentation more compelling, such as a flip chart, overhead slides, disco lights to rouse the drowsy and dry ice on hand in case the only way to settle your nerves is to simulate a fire to clear the room.

voice-jail system, *n.* Inspired by poorly designed voice-mail systems, the conversational method of the indecisive manager whose response to a problem is to enumerate an exhaustive menu of options, constructing a labyrinth of such intricacy that no one can find their way back to the original problem.

voice novel, *n.* Long-winded voice-mail message.

Vulcan nerve pinch, *n.* Contortionist juxtaposition of fingers when rebooting a PC, requiring the user to hit the control, command and return keys and the power-on button simultaneously.

vulture capital, *n.* Investor syndicates that wait patiently as capital-parched firms crawl across the desert in search of nourishing liquidity, and seize their prey before it slips into a sandy grave.

What's carnage to some is carrion to others.
 – Vancouver merchant banker Douglas Tweed, in 2001, gleeful about the crash in technology stocks

walled garden, *n.* Controlled menu of choices dictated by browser software of mobile-phone providers. Customers wishing to scale the wall must go through the trying and time-consuming process of entering a website address on the tiny number pad.

Wal-Mart has tried this, Let's see if, *phrase.* Beats doing our own research.

Wal-Mart, My research shows it worked for, *phrase.* I read it in *Department Store Age*.

wave a dead chicken, *v.* Halfhearted effort to tackle an insoluble problem – fixing a machine that is hopelessly beyond repair, for instance – in order to satisfy an insistent superior.

We merged with you because we love this company, and we have a lot to learn from you, *phrase*. You have some good assets we were able to get at a fire-sale price, and we will soon learn how to dump the rest.

weapons-grade imbecility, *n*. Term used by tech-support staff to describe slow-witted colleagues who are capable of crashing even the most rugged equipment.

weasel text, *n*. Explication for why a vaunted product will miss its launch date or must be recalled. "Adverse user experience along the compatibility dimension will be addressed with a realignment to enhance core functionality."

weeny window, *n*. Also known as "impoverished display," a low-quality screen on a handheld device that's too small and grainy to be useful.

white-glove handoff, *n*. Seamless transition. "Frank is just as thick-headed as Murray – no more, no less – so it should be a white-glove handoff."

win-win, *n*. Mutually advantageous arrangement entered into by parties who each expect to win just a little bit more than the other. In prehistory, deals were structured as "lose-lose." Cave-men clubbed each other unconscious, and no one ate well. A later innovation, "win-lose," eventually depleted the population of suckers, giving rise finally to the somewhat more accommodating spirit of modern dealmakers.

word of mouse, *n.* Sudden, widespread interest in a new product among Internet users, fanned by chat-room interlopers who talk up the product on behalf of its distributor.

workout, *n.* Fiscal fitness regime imposed on a debt-bloated company, usually by its bankers in league with opportunistic investors who have bought its shares at distress prices.

worrier, toxic, *n.* Chronic fretter who goes into a trance about everything that could go wrong. If the sufferer holds a sufficiently high station, she is a cause for paralysis not only in herself.

Xerox subsidy, *n.* On-site photocopying for private, off-site use, liberally extended to embrace "borrowing" of staplers, hole-punches, Liquid Paper and time spent using an office PC to design spiffy résumés for every job seeker in the family.

Y

yield management, *n.* In the airline business, the strategy of increasing revenue per passenger mile by cramming more seats in the cabin. This is why your knees are brushing against your chin all the way from Houston to Seattle.

Zen pose, *n.* Trancelike behavior among tech high priests who are affronted when nervy non-techies dare to query them about when profits are likely to materialize from the latest blue-sky fantasy hatched by a Bill Gates or Steve Jobs. "In the hands of a master such as Jobs, this body language can inspire employees to remarkable heights and add $5 in value to any stock," wrote *Business Week* technology columnist Joan O'C. Hamilton. "But it was hijacked during the recent dot-com run-up and successfully – if temporarily – implemented by scores of pretenders. This latter group effectively parlayed their sneers and fluency in HTML into a mystifying smokescreen for having no business competency whatsoever, all the while shaking their heads and sighing, 'You just don't get it.' If any executive of any public company has the gall to cop this attitude now, sell, sell, sell."

zero-bug release, *n.* A new software product deemed to be fit for public consumption, with all but a few hundred of the most arcane bugs removed.

zero-drag employee, *n.* Highly prized worker with no spouse, kids, pets – no ties at all – and able to toil past sundown without guilt or distraction because the workplace is home.

The perfect fund manager is a guy who can't pick his kids out in a police lineup.
  – U.S. investment consultant Michael Stolper

zero-sum expansion, *n.* An effort to expand production with no increase in physical space. In 2001, chipmaker Intel said it would boost output even as it canceled plans for 20 new office buildings around the world, which would require a cut in square footage per employee of as much as 30 percent. "This is my realm," said Andy Bryant, chief financial officer, pointing to a cubicle measuring only 9ft by 8ft. "And it is going to shrink along with everyone else's."

zero-time management, *n.* Just-in-time decision-making made possible by the unprecedented speed of data retrieval in the Internet age, enabling the modern manager to hurtle down every dark alley and make bad decisions with rapid, devastating effect.

zitcom, *n*. 1. *Variety* term for TV comedy aimed at teens. 2. Dot-com enterprise launched with money the founders raised from cutting lawns and washing cars.

zombie, *n*. Person exhibiting the attributes of the walking dead. Commonly observed among employees led by a CEO who lacks direction or is headed in too many directions; or whose employer has been subjected to a disruptive takeover, with a resulting loss of identity; or whose workplace has succumbed to a chaotic restructuring; or whose co-workers have been eliminated in a demoralizing efficiency drive; or who came *this* close to life on the outside, save for misplacing a winning lottery ticket.

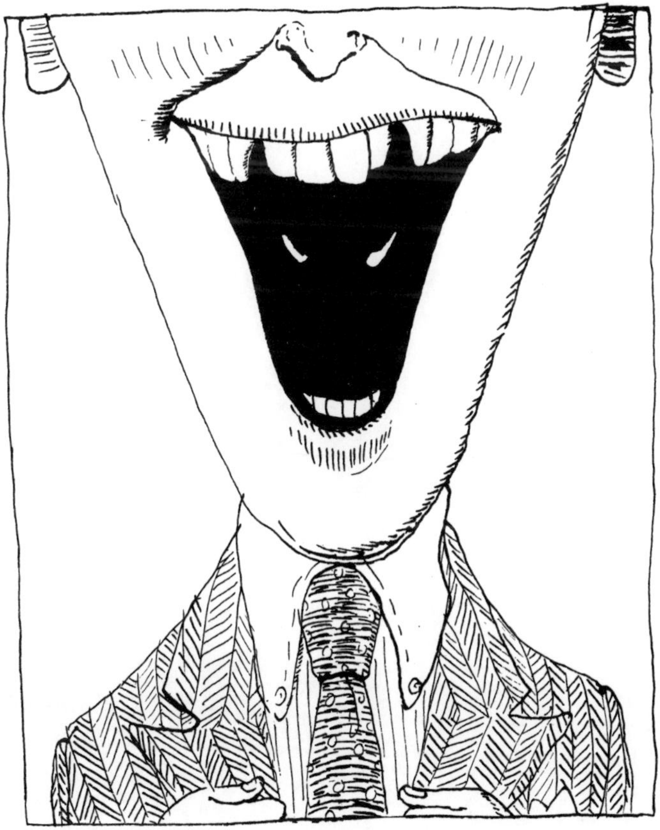

Index to Quoted Subjects

A
Adams, Scott, on value of employees, 124
Anderson, Howard, on venture capital, 178
Arbiter, Petronius, on reorganization, 139
Augustine, Norman, on synergy, 163

B
Bagehot, Walter, on bankers, 28
Balter, Lawrence, on trust slugs, 173

Benevik, Peter, on execution, 68
Barrett, Craig R., on nice-to-have's, 114
Barrett, Matthew, on bankers, 28; on customer satisfaction, 51
Barron's, on corporate charity, 125
Bennis, Warren, on playing to win, 127
Berra, Yogi, on watching, 105
Bierce, Ambrose, prefer clean English, 13
Black, Conrad, on pilfering, 152
Bonfield, Sir Peter, banal message, 27
Borman, Frank, on bankruptcy, 28
Boucicault, Dion, on time famine, 168
Bratton, David, on management concepts, 44
Brenner, Joel Glenn, on seagull managers, 148
Brill's Content, on investment bankers, 91
Brooks, David, on luxury statements, 101
Browne, Sir John, on empty gestures, 76
Bryant, Andy, on zero-sum expansion, 189
Buffett, Warren, on vacuous directors, 57; on EBITDA, 63; on forecasters, 73; on kitchen-sink accounting, 95; on tech stocks, 161

C

Churchill, Winston, on strategy, 159
Colvin, Geoffrey, on golf, 79

D

Dawson, Mark, on assumed names, 24
de Saint-Exupery, Antoine, on administrations, 167

de Talleyrand, Charles Maurice, 10
Disesa, Nina, on turnarounds, 173
Disraeli, Benjamin, on power of words, 9
Doerr, John, on starting over, 35
Drucker, Peter, on cash flow, 63; on pricing, 131
Dunlap, Al, on respect, 141

E
Edwards, Paul, on stress envy, 160
Esquire, on perks, 30

F
Fish, Stanley, on Volvo theory, 114
Flavelle, Sir Joseph, on busy directors, 57
Ford, Henry, on Ford Motor goals, 9
Fouche, Joseph, on mistakes, 67
Frank, Sergey, on Russian negotiating tactics, 77

G
Galbraith, John Kenneth, on fresh disasters, 64; on suppression of personal expression, 108; on self-restraint, 167
Gale, Thomas, on thesis vehicles, 166
Gates, Bill, on Microsoft goals, 9; on stamina, 157
Gates Sr., William, on computer language, 176
Goldbart, Stephen, on sudden wealth syndrome, 162
Goldwyn, Sam, ambiguous statement, 58
Greenberg, Herb, on EBITDA, 63

H

Halpert, Victor, on negative overshooting, 112
Haman, Gerald, on cubicle creativity, 49
Hamel, Gary, on mergers, 107
Hamilton, Joan O'C., on zen pose, 188
Hammer, Katherine, on mistakes, 39
Headlam, Bruce, on the boss's e-mail, 156
Herson, Michael, on corporate spying, 42
Hill, Chuck, on profits recessions, 132
Homer, Sidney, on investing returns, 91
Howard, Margo, on runaway e-mail, 145
Humer, Fritz, on transparency, 173
Hunt, George, on cockroach theory, 40

I

Ivester, Doug, on competing, 115

J

Jacobi, Peter, on conflicting objectives, 23
Jaswa, Raj, on energy drainers, 67

K

King, Mervyn A., on meetings, 106

L

Laflamme, Ed, on paying bills, 138
Lawrence, Rob, on dot-com work style, 55
Lenny, Richard, on meal bridging, 104
Lessin, Robert H., on angel investing, 21

Levitt Jr., Arthur, on prospectus writing, 133
Lewis, Michael, on thinking outside the box, 167
Lipton, James, on collective nouns, 115
Lowell, James Russell, on public opinion, 134
Lynch, Peter, on foolproof investing, 162

M

Machiavelli, Niccolo, words veil facts, 16
Martin, Hugh, on chipmunk mode, 39
McNealy, Scott, on investing, 32; on dress codes, 38
McSmith, Andy, on Robert Maxwell, 170
Mencken, H.L., on doing good, 125
Mitchell, James F., on stock-price targets, 131
Mobius, Mark, on dead money, 54
Molière, on pay, 88
Monaco, James, on shiss, 151

N

Neuborne, Ellen, on viral marketing, 180
Nietzsche, Friedrich, on group insanity, 121

P

Piggy, Miss, on eating, 171
Pink, Daniel H., on free agents, 74

R

Raskin, Jeff, on e-mail input, 118
Reich, Robert, on leaks, 99
Reisman, Heather, on corporate architecture, 22

Rock, John, on mission statements, 108
Rockefeller, John D., on delegating, 55
Rodgers, T.J., on videoconferencing, 179
Rosen, Harry, on recession apparel, 139
Roth, John, on legacy products, 99

S

Salter, Bill, on outsider CEOs, 119
Schlesinger, Len, on customer satisfaction, 51
Seligman, Daniel, on corporate speeches, 148
Shapiro, Eileen C., on knowledge workers, 96; on meeting ghouls, 105
Shay, R.E., on rabbit's feet, 71
Shorts, Binkley, on dead cat bounce, 54
Smith, Adam, on distorting the numbers, 62; on risk factors, 144
Stewart, Thomas A., on action training, 18
Stolper, Michael, on zero-drag employees, 189
Sunday Telegraph, on ring fencing, 143

T

Taylor, Frederick Winslow, on pay, 88
Teerlink, Rich, on empowerment, 66
Thoreau, Henry David, on mentors, 106
Tomlin, Lily, on the rat race, 160
Topkis, Maggie, on investing purity, 161
Twain, Mark, on sleepy consciences, 46
Tweed, Douglas, on vulture capital, 182
Tynan, Kevin P., on sell signals, 150

V

Varchaver, Nicholas, on tech revolutionaries, 143
Voltaire, on shooting an admiral, 162

W

Wanamaker, John, dignity for workers, 23
Wanger, Ralph, on customer service, 51
Wasserstein, Bruce, on hindsight, 82; on corporate size, 147
Webster, Daniel, world governed by appearances, 12
Welch, Jack, on customer satisfaction, 50; on downsizing, 60; on the imposter syndrome, 87; on strategic retreats, 159
Williams, Robin, on Nasdaq stocks, 32
Wolfe, Tom, on logo scrunching, 100; on paradigms, 123
Wolff, Michael, on corporate culture, 97
Wriston, Walter, on executive pay, 42; on forecasting, 73

Y

Young, Jeffrey S., on outsourcing, 147

Z

Zuckerman, Mortimer, on strategy, 160